ПНЈ

The Great Revolutions

# THE REVOLUTIONS OF LATIN AMERICA

# The Great Revolutions

J. Halcro Ferguson

# THE REVOLUTIONS OF
# LATIN AMERICA

 Thames and Hudson

© THAMES AND HUDSON LONDON 1963
PRINTED IN GREAT BRITAIN BY
EBENEZER BAYLIS AND SON LTD WORCESTER

# Contents

# Introduction: Reputation and Reality

LATIN AMERICANS are understandably touchy about the reputation of their continent for revolution and dictatorship. They complain about the apparent inability of North Americans and Europeans to distinguish between real revolutions, which have been relatively infrequent, and *putsches* or palace *coups* which have hardly affected the life of the countries in which they have occurred.

And who, they ask in effect, are other people to talk? During the century and a half since the majority of Latin American republics achieved their independence, Europe has been responsible for the start of two world wars, not to mention countless smaller conflicts, both home and colonial. Europe too, which tends to deride Latin America for its dictatorships, produced the worst of the lot—that of Adolf Hitler.

Asia and Africa have had in recent years a worse record of war and violence than Latin America. In the countries between the Río Bravo and Cape Horn there has been no parallel with the atrocities and chaos in the Congo, the activities of the OAS and the FLN in Algeria, the racial turmoil in South Africa, the communal strife after the partition of India, or the brutalities inflicted on prisoners of war taken by the Japanese. Even the most brutal of Latin American dictatorships, such as those of Pérez Jiménez in Venezuela and the late Rafael Trujillo in the Dominican Republic, have been no worse than many régimes, both past and present, in Europe itself.

Finally, Latin Americans point to the comparative stability of their frontiers. Over the last century the map of Latin America has scarcely changed. Mexico, through no fault of her own, has lost territory to the United States; Colombia, also through no fault of her own, has lost Panama. Cuba, thanks to the Spanish-American war, became independent in 1901 and Puerto Rico became a United States possession. Brazil changed

# Introduction

peacefully from Empire to Republic in 1889. There have been minor adjustments of frontiers, but few of them as the result of serious hostilities. That is all.

Over the same period Europe has seen the rise and fall of the German Empire, the disappearance of Austria-Hungary, the withdrawal of Turkey into Asia Minor, the partition of Ireland, the birth of Czechoslovakia and Yugoslavia, the numerous vicissitudes of Poland, the swallowing up of the Baltic Republics, and the placing of an Iron Curtain through the centre of the continent. Asia has seen the expansion and contraction of Japan, the withdrawal of the colonial powers, and the creation of a cluster of new states. Even more new nations are still emerging in Africa.

The
Superficial
Picture

Nevertheless the reputation of Latin America as the *enfant terrible* among continents persists. One reason for this is undoubtedly the sketchy and sensational coverage by the Press (especially in Britain) of the Latin American scene. Normal day-to-day occurrences, which would be reported as routine news if they occurred anywhere else, do not get mentioned at all if they occur in Latin America—an election will be briefly chronicled by *The Times*, but ignored by the popular Press unless someone gets shot.

This might seem to be negatived by the enormous attention given to Cuba at the time of the crisis in October 1962, when the Soviet Union set up missile bases on the island, the United States declared a blockade and threatened invasion if the missiles were not removed, and the world held its breath until the Soviet Union complied with the demand.

But in fact it was not Cuba itself which made the headlines but the two major powers: the two K's, Mr Kennedy and Mr Khrushchev, were the principal actors in the drama, while Cuba's Fidel Castro fumed impotently in the wings. As a Cuban diplomat remarked to me resignedly at the height of the crisis, 'It's out of our hands now.' It was not a Latin American *penchant* for violence and revolution which had brought the world to the brink of war but the brinkmanship of the leaders of the Soviet Union and the United States. (In fact Castro's evident powerlessness on this occasion had a considerable effect on his capacity to evoke enthusiasm or dismay in the other Latin American countries, as will be seen in the final chapter.)

Another reason for the turbulent reputation of Latin America is that, although people are aware that it is a continent composed of several countries, they unconsciously envisage it as a single entity, so that a riot in Bogotá will make them alarmed about the fate of their niece in Nicaragua. This confusion is partly a question of nomenclature. America (that is, the United States) is a single nation, South Africa is also a single nation; so, runs the false syllogism, South America must be a single nation too. This impression is strengthened by the fact that in all but two of the twenty republics Spanish is the official language—and there are people who should know better who are unaware that it is *not* spoken in Brazil and Haiti.

But all this only partially explains the common equation of Latin America with revolution. There is and long has been fire behind the obfuscating smoke, a fire which was kindled when Columbus first set foot on American soil in 1492. His discovery of a new continent was the prelude to the foundation of the first modern colonial empire, and, ever since the break-up of that empire in the first half of the nineteenth century, the Latin American countries have been going through the same process of political, economic and social adjustment, the same process of finding themselves and establishing their national identity, which the countries of Asia and Africa are going through today. The process is by no means finished yet.

It got off to a slow start in 1810 merely because it *did* start in 1810. Communications over the vast continent were vestigial, and it took weeks and months for the news of revolt to travel from its epicentres in Buenos Aires, Caracas and Mexico City. And, at a time when colonialism was still in fashion and Britain and France were only tentatively beginning to acquire overseas possessions, Spain was not lightly going to give up hers. There was no question of dominion status or of graceful withdrawal, still less of undignified scuttle. Spain fought back

A Process of
Adjustment

9

for twenty bitter years, not only impoverishing herself but preventing any progress on the part of her former colonies.

These had other problems bequeathed them by their Iberian motherlands, though Portugal left a less bitter legacy than Spain. Present-day Spanish apologists are wont to stress the undeniable positive achievements of their three centuries of rule—the founding of great cities, the spread of Christendom and European culture, the foundation of universities (those of Mexico and San Marcos in Lima both date from 1554), above all the cohesive agent of a common Castillian tongue.

Economic
Neglect

All these were of undoubted benefit to the emergent nations, but there was another side to the coin. Though the Spaniards knew their theology, and did their best to bring the blessings of Christianity to the lands they conquered, they knew nothing about economics. While it is true that Protestant historians in the nineteenth century exaggerated the lust for gold of the propagators of the faith, it is also true that the colonizers tended to value the extractive minerals above the humdrum produce of the fields. Thus it was that Lima luxuriated in the pomp of a viceregal court supported by the silver mines of Upper Peru (today Bolivia), while what is now Argentina languished for lack of the metal for which, by historical irony, the modern nation is named. So supercilious were the Spaniards about the cultivation of the soil that they allowed the irrigation system built by the Incas to fall into decay, so that the greater part of Peru which lies between the Andes and the Pacific, instead of being the nation's granary, is today a desert.

In the same way the paved highways which the Incas had built to link the provinces of their empire of Huantinsuyú were permitted to fall into desuetude and disrepair, to be rebuilt at enormous cost for motor traffic in the twentieth century. This neglect was the by-product of deliberate policy, for the Inca roads served to link one colony to another: what Spain wanted, language and religion notwithstanding, was to divide and rule; communications must run from the interior to the coast, from the coast to the mother-country. This meant in practice that when the colonies revolted they did so as individual nations, and even the immense authority of the liberators, Bolívar and San Martín, could not persuade them to unite once independence had been achieved. The divisions thus perpetuated led not only to unproductive border quarrels, but to the rise of little local autocrats who preferred bossing their own backyards to co-operating in the building up of a continent.

Finally, and most importantly from the point of view of present-day politics, the revolt which started in 1810 was what would be called today a white settlers' revolt. The Spaniards and Portuguese had never shown the same purely racial arrogance as the British, the Dutch and the Germans were later to do, nor do their descendants show it now, but Iberian society was characterized by a rigid social stratification (and still is). The metropolitan Spaniard was the social superior of the *criollo*, or locally born white, who in turn was the social superior of the *indio*. It was the *criollos* who fought the wars of independence, and despite grand phrases about equality borrowed from the French Revolution, their descendants by and large treated their inferiors more harshly than Madrid had ever allowed them to.

A 'White Settlers' Revolt

Some *indios* and more *mestizos* have subsequently risen in the social scale, but the ranks of the dispossessed have been swelled by reinforcements from elsewhere. Argentina, Uruguay, Chile and Brazil have over the years received millions of immigrants from Spain, Portugal, Italy and elsewhere. Several have been spectacularly successful, but more have joined the proletariat. In Brazil and the Caribbean the Negroes have long been emancipated from slavery, but most of them still remain at the bottom of the economic barrel, and though there is no overt discrimination (it is forbidden by law in most countries) a black skin is a social disadvantage, thus causing a latent resentment in its possessor.

The existence of all these 'under-privileged' groups has always been a danger to Latin American stability, but until recently they lacked the cohesion, the education or the leadership to make their aspirations known or their presence felt. Instead, throughout the last century and the first part of this,

Introduction

the ruling classes were able to indulge themselves in petty palace *coups* which glorified themselves by the name of revolutions and did much to create abroad the present popular image of Latin America.

But those days are over. Circumstances have combined 'to awaken the masses', in the words of one friend of mine, or 'to bring the scum to the top' (to quote another). Some of these circumstances are common to most of the world—or at any rate to the under-developed part of it—some are peculiar to Latin America. But they have combined already to produce sweeping social changes in two countries—Bolivia and Cuba —and the changes, whether peaceful or violent, will not stop there.

# Part One

## THE WINNING OF INDEPENDENCE

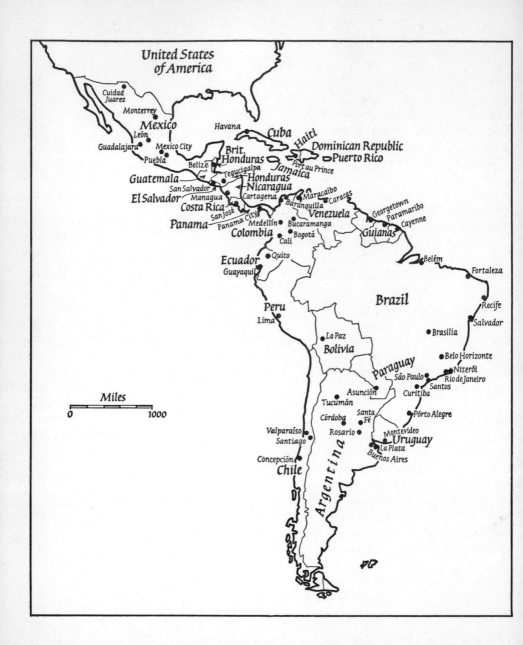

United States
of America

Cuidad
Juarez
Monterrey
Mexico
León
Guadalajara
Mexico City
Puebla
Havana
Cuba
Haiti
Dominican Republic
Puerto Rico
Brit.
Honduras
Belize
Guatemala
Tegucigalpa
Honduras
Jamaica
Port au Prince
San Salvador
Managua
Nicaragua
El Salvador
Costa Rica
San José
Cartagena
Maracaibo
Caracas
Panama
Panama City
Baranquilla
Medellín
Bucaramanga
Venezuela
Georgetown
Paramaribo
Cayenne
Colombia
Cali
Bogotá
Guianas
Ecuador
Quito
Guayaquil
Belém
Fortaleza
Peru
Lima
Brazil
Recife
Salvador
La Paz
Brasilia
Bolivia
Belo Horizonte
Niteról
Paraguay
São Paulo
Rio de Janeiro
Miles
0          1000
Asunción
Santos
Tucumán
Curitiba
Córdoba
Santa
Fé
Pôrto Alegre
Valparaíso
Rosario
Montevideo
Uruguay
Santiago
La Plata
Buenos Aires
Concepción
Argentina
Chile

# The Anti-Colonial Wars

ON 19 APRIL 1810 the City Council of Caracas, today the capital of Venezuela, escorted the newly-appointed Spanish Captain-General aboard a warship in La Guaira harbour and declared local independence of metropolitan Spain.

On 25 May 1810 the citizens of Buenos Aires, today the capital of the Argentine Republic, gathered outside the town hall, umbrellas up against a light seasonal drizzle, and demanded to know what the council was discussing and, by implication, to have a say in its deliberations.

On 16 September 1810, in the pueblo of Dolores, a Spanish Mexican priest, Father Miguel Hidalgo y Costilla, started on a protest march to Mexico City at the head of four thousand dissatisfied *indios*, *mestizos* and *criollos*.

These three relatively unspectacular events, occurring thousands of miles apart, marked the beginning of the end of the Spanish American empire, and the start of a war which, in the prematurely optimistic words of a British Foreign Secretary, George Canning, was to bring 'a new world into existence to redress the balance of the old'.

What was it that linked the *porteños* of Buenos Aires on the edge of the flat pampas, the *caraqueños* four thousand feet up from the tropical Caribbean, and the inhabitants of wild, majestic Mexico, in a common dissatisfaction so great as to make them oppose their puny resources to the might of a nation from which most of them had originally sprung?

At that time there was little or no contact between the various Viceroyalties, Captaincies-General and Audiencias which comprised the Spanish Empire in the New World. Like Ghana and Nigeria or Dahomey and Cameroun in the twentieth century, they had closer ties with Europe than they did with each other. And, unlike the modern African colonies, they were not bound by a feeling of racial outrage or encouraged by any concept of a continental personality. In everything but

A Common
Concern

15

geography most of those with the influence to stage a protest still considered themselves as Spaniards, albeit Spaniards in America, and were divided neither by language nor religion from the mother-country.

British historians have tended to find the seeds of revolt in the economic dependence of the colonies, in the laws which restricted their trade to the Iberian Peninsula, and this explanation is understandable enough: Britain, as a maritime nation, suffered herself from these restrictions and naturally sympathized with merchants in the Americas who found them irksome too. The first British history books to deal with the subject were written in Victorian times when a materialistic view of history (except of course one's own glorious history) was a natural one to take. Karl Marx, the proponent of dialectical materialism, was after all a Victorian.

North American historians, equally naturally, have tended to lay more stress on the lack of democracy in the Spanish colonies, the resentment of the colonists at the domination of Madrid, the fact that the highest posts in all the colonies were reserved for those born in what Latin Americans still call the *madre patria*. They mentally equate the *criollo* revolt with the Boston Tea Party and the demand for 'no taxation without representation'. And with their own deliberate decision to replace the monarchy with republican institutions. This view, though, like the British one, it has some validity, represents a false analogy.

The *criollos*, outside intellectual circles, did not yearn for a democratic system which they had never known, and would probably not have liked if they had experienced it. In many cases their opposition to Spanish rule was motivated less by lofty idealism than by resentment at Madrid's paternalistic efforts to get them to treat 'their' *indios* properly. But their very human objection to peninsular Spaniards being promoted over their heads undoubtedly did play a very large part in alienating them from their traditional allegiance—though it is only fair to say that the *cabildos coloniales*, or local municipal councils, did in fact enjoy very considerable powers.

They also lay great stress on the effect on thinking people in the colonies of the French and North American Revolutions. Of these, the French Revolution of 1789 had by far the greater influence. As Latins, they were far closer to France than to Britain's thirteen dissident colonies to the north. Regardless of politics, France was the source of their culture, and indeed remained so until well on into the twentieth century. The generation of upper-class Latin Americans to whom French was a required second language is only just dying out, and up till recently well-bred Argentine children believed that babies, like everything else Mamá bought, came from Paris.

Certainly the ideas which helped to spark off the wars of independence came from France: writers like Rousseau and Voltaire, prohibited by the Spanish authorities (whose views on desirable reading-matter have not changed much), were smuggled into the Americas and read in secrecy like copies of *Lady Chatterley* in a girls' boarding school. The French Revolution itself, too far away to frighten liberals as it frightened Edmund Burke in England, made an instant appeal with its call for liberty, equality and fraternity. Latin Americans love magnificent generalizations and rousing phrases (Churchill was their hero in World War II as much for his oratory as his actions), and if the French had not invented the triple slogan some South American would have had to do it for them. It is not without significance that the party songs of the Liberals in Colombia and APRA in Peru are both set to the tune of *La Marseillaise*, and almost all Latin American national anthems are reminiscent of it, both in sound and sense.

France was not the only European country to have an effect on the fathers of Latin American independence. Britain, too, played its part—sometimes in a roundabout way. In 1806, a British force under Admiral Sir Home Popham landed at Quilmes, now a suburb of Buenos Aires, and occupied the capital. The Spanish Viceroy, Sobremonte, withdrew prudently to Córdoba in the foothills of the Andes, but the British were ejected by the *criollos* themselves under the command of the Frenchman Liniers, in an engagement known to

Argentines as the 'Reconquista'. In the following year another British force, under General Whitelocke, made a second attempt at invasion, but was repulsed without taking the city in what is now known as the 'Defensa'.

The British surprise at this reverse can be gauged by the fact that the British Embassy in Buenos Aires possesses a book published in 1806 entitled *The New Colony of Buenos Ayres*. But it was nothing to the surprise and gratification of the *criollos*. It taught them, in the first place, that they could not rely on the protection of the Spaniards, and in the second place that they could do without it. Furthermore, contact with British officers, with their freedom to read and discuss what they liked, made *porteños* realize what a narrow and restricted life they had been leading. Both these reactions paved the way for the unprecedented outburst of 1810.

But Britain's part in fomenting the liberating revolution was not a purely negative one. Successive British governments, intermittently at war with Spain, saw in the dissatisfaction of the American colonies a stick with which to beat their perennial rivals (somewhat in the same way as the United States and the Soviet Union try to manipulate 'uncommitted' countries today). And the 'Precursor of Independence', the Venezuelan Francisco Miranda, spent many years in London, lobbying His Majesty's Government and gathering round him sympathizers with his cause; while the revered liberators, Simón Bolívar of Venezuela and José de San Martín of Argentina, both lived for a considerable period in Britain. When hostilities broke out, a British legion fought for Bolívar in Venezuela and Colombia; the Argentine Navy was founded by Admiral Brown of County Mayo, Ireland; the Chilean Navy by Admiral Lord Cochrane (also responsible for the glengarries worn by Brazilian marines); and an Irishman called Bernardo O'Higgins became Chile's first Chief of State.

From a purely military point of view, Spain herself nurtured the soldiers who fought against her. San Martín had been trained in a Spanish military academy and served with distinction in Europe and North Africa. There is a modern parallel in the ALN officers in Algeria who once fought for France, and, had Britain not relinquished India when she did, many former Sandhurst cadets might similarly have been leading Indian rebel forces. The discipline and solidarity which Latin American armies still possess owe much to the discipline and *esprit de corps* instilled in colonial soldiers by the motherland they repudiated.

The colonial revolt of the Americas in 1810 exhibits all the contradictory elements of such movements today—the mixture of mercenary and idealistic motives; the ambiguous love-hate relationship towards the colonial power; the uneasy alliance between soldiers and intellectuals; the foreign backing granted for extraneous reasons; the participation of outsiders fired by the love of liberty or merely by the spirit of adventure or hope of quick rewards. And, as usual, the mute sufferings of the simple people, subject to impressments, requisitioning, reprisals, constant uncertainty, and the destruction of their homes and property—if any.

Contradictory elements

Those of the population who were white or *mestizo* could console themselves with the thought that when the wars were over they could come into their inheritance, or at least return to a not too disagreeable *status quo ante*. They could respond to the idea that after independence they would be citizens of a new nation with its own flag, its own institutions, its own anthem, its own heroes. They could cheer the news of the battles of Carabobo and Boyacá, Chacabuco and Maipú, as Bolívar marched from the north and San Martín from the south to meet at Guayaquíl in Ecuador in 1822.

For the *indios*, who kept alive the memory of the Aztec Empire (a cruel culture, but their own), there was no such silver lining, except in Mexico where they had preserved some dignity. The *indios*, then as now, formed the greater part of the population of Peru, Ecuador, Colombia and Central America, and at that time still existed in large numbers in Argentina and Uruguay, but they scarcely mattered in what was in effect a war between whites. Some, like the plainsmen of Patagonia and the jungle-dwellers of Amazonas, had not yet been affected by a European colonization. Some, like the Caribs and the Arawaks of the Antilles, had already been exterminated. The rest, from the comparatively sophisticated Quéchuas to the most primitive tribes, had been largely reduced to virtual serfdom in exchange for more or less adequate instruction in the Christian faith.

Bolívar, it is true, preached the equality of all born in the Americas, but he was hardly heeded by the great mass of the colonists, while San Martín, by the standards of his time an exemplary man, had no hesitation in impressing Indian slaves to swell the ranks of his liberating army. As for the Negroes, who had been imported from Africa to do the work for which the *criollos* were too grand and the *indios* too unco-operative, their emancipation was declared in almost all the former colonies. But, since they were landless and penniless, freedom availed them nothing, and mostly they were obliged to remain in menial jobs to keep themselves alive.

Progress is
retarded

This perpetuation of an outmoded social system was one of the two major factors which were to retard the progress of Latin America until the present day. The other was the total failure to construct a successful constitutional and political system which would answer the needs of a huge, under-populated, under-educated, under-developed, geographically divided continent. Most countries took their ideals from France and their institutions from the United States, though the French Revolution had been succeeded by Napoleon and Napoleon by a Bourbon Restoration, and the institutions which suited the closely-knit colonies of North America had little relevance to the lands to the south of it.

One of the North American institutions which proved entirely disastrous was the Presidential system, which divorced the executive from the legislature and in effect, though not in theory, left all real authority in the hands of the former.

Latin Americans are brilliant at concocting constitutions but they are less than brilliant in their attempts to make them work. Bolívar himself wrote Bolivia's constitution in 1824, but for fifty years it was more honoured in the breach than in the observance, and has since been superseded several times. The reason is that, though Bolívar was a soldier by profession, he was still an intellectual by inclination, and, like all Latin American intellectuals of the period, influenced by the ideas of the age of reason and the perfectibility of man.

Unfortunately for the founders of the republics, men turned out to be unreasonable and, if perfectible, still far from perfect. While earnest and public-spirited people penned utopian rules of national conduct, events made nonsense of their efforts. Small wonder that in the circumstances the 'haves' consolidated their hold over the 'have-nots', the landowners in the interior ignored the laws promulgated in the capital, the demobilized local levies resorted to banditry, and the armies—the only disciplined elements in the population—became the only effective forces in the new nations.

In the conditions then obtaining this last factor was not only inevitable but for the time being desirable, for without the armies the new nations would have lapsed into Congolese chaos. But in the long run the effects were far from salutary. The soldiers were, with some exceptions, uninterested in political theory or constitutional niceties: they saw their job as one of maintaining stability and order. They therefore tended to support any civilian group, however self-interested or reactionary, which seemed capable of exercising some sort of authority.

When this authority became repressive enough to cause serious discontent, the military threw their weight behind the most likely rival, thus causing endless changes of government, devaluing the reputations of the new republics, and prolonging into the twentieth century the power of oligarchies belonging to the eighteenth.

# Challenge of Freedom

BRAZIL IS THE LARGEST COUNTRY on the American continent, if one excludes Alaska and the empty Arctic from the United States and Canada respectively. It occupies half of the land area of South America, but it is divided from its neighbours by language and history and to a great extent by geography, and much of the foregoing chapter does not apply to it.

The linguistic and historical differences are the fortuitous result of a Papal Bull issued in 1493 by Pope Alexander VI who, needless to say, had never set foot in the Americas. This Bull, whose purpose was to avoid conflict between the Christian nations in the newly discovered continent, provided that all territory to the east of a line drawn 375 leagues eastwards from Cape Verde should belong to Portugal and all territory to the west to Spain. This was confirmed by the two countries in the Treaty of Tordesillas in the following year, so that when, in 1500, the Portuguese navigator Pedro Alvares Cabral first sighted the Brazilian coast he was able to claim a vast area (later to be considerably increased) for the Portuguese crown.

Brazil grows up in Isolation From the first, Brazil, which owes its name to a tree known as *palo brasil*, grew up in isolation from, and in different circumstances to, the Spanish colonies in the hemisphere. In the first place it lacked the autochthonous civilizations which proved a challenge to the Spaniards in Peru and Mexico and provided problems for future generations. In the second place it did not appear to possess the precious metals which filled the *conquistadores* with dreams of wealth and glory. Huge tracts of its territory consisted of jungle or inhospitable scrubland.

It was not an area to excite enthusiasm in Iberian breasts, so that casual demarcation and almost accidental discovery were followed by unwilling settlement. The Portuguese authorities, in fact, treated their new possession as Britain originally treated Australia, as a useful dumping ground for people who

22

were not wanted at home, notably criminals and Jews, later augmented by involuntary arrivals in the shape of shipwrecked sailors. In the absence of other womenfolk these men took wives (often more than one) from the nomadic Indian tribes who were the only original inhabitants, thus starting the process of miscegenation which has characterized Brazil ever since.

So little did the Portuguese bother about Brazil that it was not until 1530 that Lisbon finally established a formal government in the colony. But the first official emissary, Martím Affonso de Souza, sent back such a gloomy report both of the poor possibilities of the country and the difficulties of defending it, that the Portuguese government decided that Brazil was too much trouble and turned it over to private enterprise, dividing it into fifteen strips running from the coast to the Tordesillas line, whose administration was entrusted to private Portuguese citizens. (An interesting parallel is afforded by later British governments which left the development of large parts of the Empire to chartered companies.) This measure was one of the factors which contributed to the present federal structure of Brazil.

In 1549 it was superseded by what was on paper a more conventional colonial system, but by then the regional pattern had been well established, and the real authority of the Governors General (later Viceroys) did not in practice extend much beyond the area of their immediate administration around São Salvador de Baía, while the Portuguese authorities paid much less attention to Brazil as a whole than the Spanish government did to any one of its transatlantic possessions.

This was not the only difference between the development of the Spanish and Portuguese colonies. Though Spain's dominions were intermittently harassed by English attacks on shipping and even the sacking of coastal cities, they were not subject to serious outside interference until the British invasions of 1806 and 1807.

Brazil had a far harder time of it. The French actually established a colony on Brazilian soil in 1555 and were not

Foreign
intervention

expelled until 1567, after they had been weakened by internal squabbles between Catholics and Calvinists. Later in the century a group of French Huguenots settled on the north coast and were not expelled until 1615—the fight for their removal being partly responsible for the beginning of Brazil's expansion northward. In the meantime metropolitan neglect of Brazil had become more marked as a result of Spain's occupation of Portugal in 1580 and the Spanish-Portuguese war of 1640–88 which restored Portuguese sovereignty.

By now the Dutch had replaced the French as the principal foreign interlopers. They took Olinda and Recife in 1630 and within a decade the Dutch West India Company controlled the whole of the north of Brazil, and Prince Maurits van Nassau had been sent as governor. Portugal, at war with Spain at home, could do nothing to assist the colony, and the Brazilians, like the Argentines at the time of the Reconquista and the Defensa, had to fend for themselves, eventually expelling the Dutch, who were by then at war with England, in 1661. This victory not only served, like the Reconquista and the Defensa, to stiffen local patriotism and self-confidence, but also brought together all races and classes of Brazilians in a common cause, giving them a sense of nationhood which the Spanish colonies did not achieve, even as separate units, until much later.

The foreign contribution to Brazilian development was not confined to armed intervention. In the commercial field Lisbon was a good deal more lenient than Madrid in allowing its overseas subjects to trade with outsiders. It was, furthermore, far less efficient in enforcing the restrictions which it did impose, with the result that in the eighteenth century it is estimated that almost half of Brazil's trade was with Britain while a great deal of the rest, despite hostilities, was with France and the Netherlands.

Negro slavery

The pattern of settlement, foreign wars and trade were not the only factors which differentiated Brazil from her Spanish-speaking neighbours. Although the Spaniards, like everyone else, had imported African slaves into their Caribbean colonies, Negro slavery was not a vital factor in the economy of Spain's other territories. In Brazil, thanks to the unsuitability and unwillingness of the Indians, it was. No reliable figures of racial composition exist for the earlier colonial period, but in 1818 the explorer Alexander von Humboldt estimated Brazil's population at 1,887,500 Negroes, 843,000 Whites, and 628,000 people of mixed race (his figure for the Indians, which is a good deal lower than seems probable, must have been based on pure guesswork). Not all the Negroes remained as slaves and many of the *mestiços* and *mamelucos* were recognized by their European fathers and achieved some social recognition, so that although in Brazil there was, as there still is, a huge distance between the top and the bottom of the social and economic structure, there did exist a considerable middle class which in the Spanish-speaking countries was largely lacking. Furthermore, though many slave-owners were undoubtedly brutal, others were paternalistic, and by the standards of the times even enlightened. This was true of very few if any of the Spanish *encomenderos*, though the *indios* who worked for these were not officially slaves. The Church in Brazil too, particularly the Jesuit order, had a fitfully beneficial effect on the treatment of the subject races, at any rate in the north of the country: to the south the thrustful *Paulistas* paid little attention to the priests as they pushed ruthlessly forward into the hinterland.

The remaining great difference between Brazil's situation and that of her neighbours lay in her relationship with the Crown. The Kings of Spain tended to be remote figures, preoccupied not only with more American possessions than they could conveniently compass, but also with extensive European commitments. The Braganças, who ruled Portugal, were far closer—even geographically—to their transatlantic territory, and the link became stronger still when in 1824 Napoleon invaded and occupied Portugal.

The Portuguese Prince Regent, Dom João, accompanied by the entire royal family, sailed for Brazil under the protection of the British fleet. Once installed in Rio de Janeiro he instituted numerous reforms including the long overdue installation of

The Crown

Brazil's first printing press, and when in 1821 he was able to return to Portugal as King João VI he left his son Pedro behind as Viceroy. The Lisbon parliament, however, looked with disfavour on the new freedoms of its former colony, and ordered Dom Pedro home. Dom Pedro declined to go, and on the 7 September 1822 he declared Brazil independent, becoming himself the Emperor Dom Pedro I Thus Brazil became the only American nation apart from Canada to achieve its independence without war and to perpetuate the institution of monarchy, an accidental achievement which has had a great effect in the formation of the Brazilian national character.

Though the new monarch had made such a popular move he did not have an easy time of it. Having granted the country a relatively liberal constitution, he was faced with insurrection and republicanism at home, while abroad, his country, which had been so buffeted by overseas nations, became embroiled with its neighbours; in the first instance in a war with Argentina over the control of the territory known as the Banda Oriental (East Bank) of the Uruguay.

\*     \*     \*     \*

Uruguay's
birth-pangs

Uruguay, today the most pacific and democratic of the South American nations, had birth-pangs as violent as any of them. As part of the Spanish Viceroyalty of the Río de la Plata (itself long disputed with Portugal), Uruguay, like Buenos Aires, was attacked by the British in 1806 and British troops occupied Montevideo in 1807.

When Buenos Aires declared its independence in 1810, the Spanish governor of the Banda Oriental refused to recognize the new authority and asked for Portuguese help. A *gaucho* leader, José Gervasio Artígas, became the head of the Uruguayan resistance and offered his services to the governing *junta* in Buenos Aires. The *junta*, however, regarded itself as heir to the whole Viceroyalty, while the Orientales wanted an independent Uruguay, so that when the Argentines found themselves hard pressed by the Spaniards elsewhere they abandoned Artígas.

26

For the next seventeen years the unfortunate Uruguayans found themselves fighting the Spaniards, the Portuguese, and their successors the Brazilians, and for five of those years Uruguay was administered as a Brazilian province. At last, in 1828, largely thanks to British mediation, the República Oriental del Uruguay was recognized as an independent nation, but once the external threat was removed the Uruguayans fell to fighting among themselves, and something like civil war raged intermittently for nearly a century.

Though there was supposed to be a democratic republican constitution, it remained a dead letter and the Presidency was occupied by whichever of the two warring bands, the *Blancos* and the *Colorados*, held the capital city. Today these bands have become respectable political parties, but at that period they had about as much ideological differentiation as the similarly named contenders in the Wars of the Roses—indeed Uruguay in the nineteenth century resembled nothing so much as England in the fifteenth. One President, Colonel Latorre (two of whose predecessors had been assassinated), found the whole thing too much for him and resigned, declaring that the Uruguayans were ungovernable.

*      *      *      *

Uruguay was not the only small neighbour with whom Brazil found herself embroiled. (In 1852–53 Brazil was also engaged with a powerful neighbour, the dictator Rosas of the Argentine Republic.) Far more serious was the fantastic war (1864–70) between Brazil, Argentina and Uruguay on the one side, and tiny, land-locked Paraguay on the other. This extraordinary interlude had nothing to do with the post-revolutionary ferment which was agitating the other American nations, but it had such a profound effect on the future of Paraguay—up till today—that it cannot be ignored.

The Guaraní-speaking Indians of Paraguay, a warrior nation, never admitted that they were conquered by the Spaniards— they absorbed them. Spanish men married Guaraní girls and the children were brought up speaking Guaraní so that today

The
Paraguayan
War

27

the greater part of the nation is *mestizo* and everyone, including the few pure whites, speaks Guaraní, though there are some who do not speak Spanish. Thus, when the wars of independence came, the Paraguayans regarded themselves as entitled to revert to their former independence, and paid no attention to politicians in Buenos Aires who thought that Paraguay should join the Argentine confederation merely because it had formed part of the Viceroyalty of the Río de la Plata. To the Paraguayans the Viceroyalty was an ephemeral institution and of no concern to them: they lived their lives in their own way.

But this isolationism soon became an almost insane nationalism, which reached its apogee under the dictatorship of Marshal Francisco Solano López. In 1864, irritated by his enormous Brazilian neighbour, he went to war with her. In order to reach southern Brazil he sent his troops by a short cut across the Argentine province of Corrientes. The Argentines, not unnaturally, objected and declared war, as did Uruguay, which was tied by treaty to Brazil.

This incredibly unequal conflict (as if Belgium were to take on France, Germany and Denmark) lasted for six years, at the end of which, out of half a million Paraguayans, less than a quarter of a million survived, the majority of them women and children. López himself, accidentally but mortally wounded on capture, is reported to have said, *Yo muero con mi patria*—'I die with my country', and he was very nearly right. Yet today he is a national hero. Other Latin Americans, though they think the Paraguayans individually charming, find them collectively a little hard to understand.

\*   \*   \*   \*

Brazilian
progress

In Brazil meanwhile, despite the war (which for most Brazilians had been almost as remote as the Zulu or Ashanti wars were to the British, if rather more costly), Dom Pedro II had succeeded to the throne—in 1840—and life was comparatively peaceful, prosperous and progressive under his surveillance.

Foreign trade, in what was after all the Brazilian tradition, was encouraged. Immigration, not only from Portugal but from Italy, Germany and other countries, was fostered and brought with it new skills, new enthusiasms and a further diversification of Brazil's racial and cultural heritage. Communications improved: Dom Pedro installed for his own use the first telephone line between Rio and the summer capital of Petropolis, and formally helped to haul in the first cable to link Europe with South America, laid by a British company.

Of course, all was not perfect in this saga of success. Education lagged behind so that millions were illiterate. Communications were confined largely to the cities of the south; the interior, plagued by tropical diseases for which there were as yet no cure, remained romantic and inaccessible. But one great human advance was made: slavery was abolished in 1888—largely through the influence of the royal family—and because the problem had been tackled by piecemeal legislation over the years, emancipation caused neither the economic disruption which resulted in Jamaica nor the bitterness which still endures in the United States.

It may seem ungrateful that in the following year the Brazilians decided to dispense with the monarchy, but the possession of a royal régime was regarded askance in the rest of the Americas and the Emperor abdicated amicably and proceeded peacefully to Portugal, on board the British vessel *Magdalena* of the Royal Mail Line.

Today there are still streets and railway stations in Brazil named after Dom Pedro II; and his descendants, including the putative Pretender to the throne, live once more in Brazil. The Republic of the United States of Brazil has the satisfaction of recalling that it achieved its independence, emancipated its slaves, and changed from a monarchy to a republic without resort to arms. And that is a triple record few, if any, nations can compete with.

\*　　\*　　\*　　\*

Brazil, despite its differences of language and development, is, and always has been, part of the mainstream of Latin American history and culture. This is not true of Haiti, which would

Haiti

29

serve as a text-book example for anyone wanting to make out a case for the unmitigated evil of colonialism. Rather than Java or Ceylon, it might have served for the island 'where every prospect pleases and only man is vile'—if by man one means the exploiter rather than the exploited.

Although the island of Hispaniola, of which Haiti occupies the western end, was originally discovered by Christopher Columbus, it was rapidly and unofficially taken over by the French. These Frenchmen were not dispatched by any orders from Paris but were pirates and buccaneers who infiltrated from Tortuga on Haiti's northern coast. Most of them were Normans and partly responsible for the Créole dialect which almost all Haitians speak at home today.

These French squatters were among the worst of white settlers with one exception; they were not particularly colour-prejudiced. They imported slaves who happened to be black but they would equally have imported slaves of any other colour if they had happened to be available. When they slept with slave women they recognized the resultant mulatto progeny, sent them to France to be educated, and founded the *métis* race which now constitutes the *élite*, the upper class of Haiti.

This liberalism towards their own offspring did not preclude a different attitude towards other slaves who were beaten up and sold whenever it suited their masters. These latter enjoyed a standard of living, based on the servitude of the sugar estates, not only higher than that of most of their coevals in the Americas, but at least on a level with the most favoured citizens of metropolitan France. Like the *pieds noirs* in Algeria, the whites of Haiti came to believe themselves destined by providence to occupy a privileged position in the alien territory where they had settled, and Saint Domingue, as it was known, was called the brightest jewel in the French Imperial crown.

It was certainly bright for the people at the top, but it was not at all bright for those dependent upon them. In 1791 the black slaves, who, despite illiteracy and persecution, valued their human dignity as much as anyone else, rose in revolt under a brilliant leader, Toussaint l'Ouverture, who is insufficiently appreciated in the country of his birth. He subsequently died in prison in France, the country whose revolution had sparked off the very revolt he himself had started in the belief that *liberté, égalité et fraternité* applied equally to black and brown people as to white.

Napoleon held different ideas, and even before his assumption of power the white Haitian lobby had managed to dissuade the government of Republican France from extending the benefits of the revolution to the majority of the citizens of Haiti. Their reactionary attitude was helped by the division between the Haitian slaves and the black and brown *affranchis*, the descendants of freed slaves who had been granted civil rights by the French monarchy and achieved a kind of middle-class status. The *affranchis* in fact might well have joined *les jaunes*, as Haitians called the whites, in setting up an independent state run by the privileged minority, had not white superiority borne down heavily on freeman and slave alike.

As a result, in 1804, the *affranchis*, mostly concentrated in the south, and the slaves, who were more potent in the north, joined together to expel the whites, who not surprisingly were subjected to the same savage treatment which they had meted out to their slaves and social inferiors. Those who survived fled to France, Trinidad and Venezuela, and Haiti became the first independent Negro nation in the modern world.

Expulsion
of the
Whites

But independence brought neither happiness nor good government. The colonial system had effectively divided the *affranchis* from the slaves, so that the former became a literate *élite* while the latter became soldiers, the only trade for which their lack of education fitted them in the days before armies became mechanized and scientific. So great was this division that from 1807 to 1820 the North was ruled separately by the black Emperor Christophe while the South became an independent republic under *élite* presidents.

This division was temporary, but one effect of colonial rule was to prove permanent—the inability of the remaining population to maintain the economic structure of the country. This had been dependent on the labour of the large estates which were the only units capable of producing sugar, coffee or indeed most of the products whose exports had made Haiti viable. The *élite* had been educated into believing that manual labour was beneath their dignity; the slaves regarded independence as an opportunity to escape the barrack-like life of the estates and to set up their own smallholdings. Successive Haitian governments tried to remedy this situation by enforced collectivization or by encouraging the newly-liberated peasant farmers to form co-operatives, but they failed.

The glorious revolution which has produced such national heroes as Toussaint and Dessalines ground to a halt in the face of the stubborn resistance of the ordinary people to any form of organization and the equally marked reluctance of the *élite* to follow any but gentlemanly pursuits. (There are signs that *uhuru* in Africa today is producing similar results on the departure of colonial authority, even though modern colonial powers have set a far better example than France did in Haiti and have fostered education rather than discouraged it.)

Élite
Government

From 1820 to 1843 Haiti was in the hands of the *élite* under President Boyer. Engaged in intellectual argument *à la française*, they let Haiti slip into lethargy and isolation. She was boycotted by the Roman Catholic Church whose white priests had been massacred during the revolution; her roads fell into disrepair because it was nobody's business to maintain them; houses collapsed for lack of builders and masons; the estates were in ruins and foreign trade was at a standstill.

With Boyer's death the black-dominated, largely illiterate army took over, and ran the country with startling and sometimes comical inefficiency for the rest of the century. The façade of democracy was a farce. In the seventy-one years between 1843 and 1914 there were twenty presidents, almost none of them properly elected and few of them destined to serve their full term, and in one lunatic interlude Haiti had another self-styled Emperor who only served to make the country a laughing stock for the rest of the world.

This tragic story has often been used to prove that Negroes are incapable of governing themselves, but this has no more validity than President Latorre's similar conclusion about his Uruguayan fellow-countrymen, which has since proved to be so wrong. What it does show is that not only the wheat but also the tares planted by colonial powers are only too likely to be reaped by the inhabitants of the countries where they were sown.

# The Nineteenth Century and After

To MOST EUROPEANS the nineteenth century was a period of industrial revolution or of the achievement of national identity, or in some cases—notably that of Germany—both.

In Latin America it was neither. National identity in the case of the great majority of countries had been achieved even before independence, and in Mexico, Peru and Paraguay it had a tradition to feed on which went back to before the conquest and which was somewhat smugly accepted by the conquerors, in rather the same way as Norman invaders became English, or second generation Poles and Czechs in the United States tacitly take on the mantle of George Washington and Thomas Jefferson.

The industrial revolution, on the other hand, never touched the American continent south of the Río Bravo. There were many reasons for this, but chief among them was a state of perpetual political unrest coupled with an almost total lack of real social development. Both these factors militated against the establishment of any kind of industry and deterred foreign capitalists from large-scale investment.

Argentina

This was initially true even of what was later in the century to become the most progressive of Latin American nations, Argentina. The end of the war of independence brought no peace to the Argentine Confederation, which even during the war had suffered from the mutual distrust and rivalry between Buenos Aires and the other provinces, between the traders of the city and the *gauchos* of the *pampa*. This division between federalists and *unitarios* (or centralists) led almost immediately to intermittent civil war culminating in the dictatorship from 1828 to 1852 of Juan Manuel Rosas—ironically a federalist.

Rosas' dictatorship, however, though as brutal as any the continent has known, did have one beneficial effect: at whatever cost, it established internal peace and conditioned the Argentine people not only to regard such tranquillity as normal but to accept it as a prerequisite of dignified national life. The national anthem continued to proclaim, 'Crowned with glory let us live, else we swear with glory to die', but Argentines became less and less inclined to die, with glory or otherwise.

Consequently, when the *unitario* General Urquiza defeated Rosas at the battle of Monte Caseros in 1852, the country accepted the change-over peacefully, and when Bartólome Mitre became President ten years later, he accepted the 1853 compromise constitution which, to placate the federalists, allowed considerable latitude to the provinces, realizing that to do otherwise would only lead to another civil war which no one wanted. Bartólome Mitre, victor of the Paraguayan war, university professor, translator of Dante, founder of the great newspaper *La Nación*, can be considered the founder of modern Argentina.

The peaceful and constitutional era his presidency ushered in had an immediate effect on the country's development. Immigrants poured in from poverty-stricken Italy, hungry Ireland, and even from the more prosperous countries of Europe. British investors who had had their eye on the Río de la Plata ever since 1806, despite the many setbacks of intervening years, took heart again. In Mitre's first year of office the Province of Buenos Aires granted to a British company the concession for building and operating a railway over the seventy-two-mile stretch from Buenos Aires to Chascomús, the first strand in a vast network which was soon to stretch from Buenos Aires northwards to Bolivia, westwards over the Andes to Chile, and southwards towards Patagonia.

*Economic and Social Development*

The establishment of rapid communication with the remote interior transformed the entire economy of the country, making it possible to transport cattle swiftly to the capital. In 1882 the first *frigorífico*, or meat-freezing plant, was established by Eugenio Terrasón in Buenos Aires, and Argentina's biggest industry, the export of beef, principally to Britain, came into existence.

In the social sphere also, Argentine developed fast. President Domingo Faustino Sarmiento (1868–74) laid the foundations of universal education, and brought in teachers from the United States to speed up its implementation. President Roque Sáenz Peña (1912–16), inheriting a largely literate population, introduced the secret ballot and universal adult male suffrage. Subsequent elections, won—after a long period of conservative rule—by Hipólito Irigoyen of the left-wing *Unión Cívica Radical*, established a two-party system and started for Argentina a system of democratic government which lasted until 1930.

Unfortunately, however, social progress did not keep pace with political advice, with subsequent results which are still bedevilling Argentina today.

Tranquil
Chile

Across the Andes, Chile had almost as turbulent a start in independent life as Argentina, but it did not last long, and from 1831 onwards Chile knew more internal tranquillity than almost any other Spanish-American country. For thirty years she had a succession of conservative presidents, ruling largely in the interests of the land-owning oligarchy, it is true, but honest and capable. From 1861 onwards Chilean administrations tended to be more liberal, but they maintained equally strong and centralized governments, so that Chile was spared the constant friction between the capital and the provinces which held back Argentina for so many years. Her only foreign war (1879–84), with Peru and Bolivia, resulted in complete victory for Chile, which briefly occupied Peru and permanently annexed Bolivia's only sea-coast, including the port of Arica.

At the end of the century Chile experienced her only civil war, between supporters of a strong presidency and believers in the final authority of parliament. The latter won. In view of the many instances of abuse of authority by Latin American chief executives, this might be considered a good thing. In fact, however, whatever the theoretical virtues of a parliamentary system, in practice in Chile it gave birth to a multiplicity of parties. Constant shifting of political alliances, and a series of short-lived coalitions, made the office of presidency so disagreeable that from then on only a minority of presidents have served their full term, the rest having retired, gone sick, had nervous breakdowns, or even died.

As a result Chilean governments were too weak to deal adequately with the grave problems affecting the country: the loss of the market for nitrates, one of her two principal products, due to the discovery of artificial fertilizers; the fluctuating price of copper, her other principal commodity; the drift from the country to the cities, a problem Chile shares with almost all Latin American nations; an out-of-date agricultural system, in which a tiny proportion of the population owns a high proportion of the land, and which has led to revolutions elsewhere; and a constantly rising cost of living. On paper the picture looks so frightening that one can but conclude that only the extraordinary good nature of the Chileans has prevented the country being plunged into a blood-bath long ago—though perhaps the prevalence of sometimes catastrophic earthquakes discourages them from bringing any other disasters upon themselves.

*    *    *    *

Bolivia

But if Argentina and Chile had their troubles in the nineteenth and early twentieth centuries, the Andean nations to the north were in a far sorrier plight, and of them Bolivia had the worst time of all. The bleak *altiplano*, 13,000 feet above sea level, where most Bolivians live, is in itself so inhospitable that one wonders why the Quéchuas and Aymaras ever chose to live there, and why the Spaniards bothered to follow them up, silver mines or no. It is another world from the smiling fields of central Chile or the rich *pampas* of Argentina, and as befits another world it has another history.

In the first place, unlike the two coastal countries, Bolivia, not surprisingly, never attracted much European settlement, either before or after independence, though this did not prevent the Europeans who had settled there from taking possession of both the land and the government. And if in some parts of the world European minorities can justify such action on the grounds that the natives are unfit to rule themselves, in Bolivia such a claim would be laughable. The natives had been ruling themselves, and when they ceased to do so Alto Perú (as it was then called) was ultimately controlled by Madrid. Subsequent white settler domination provided probably the most inefficient governments to which any country has been subjected in modern history.

In the chaotic period following independence General Andrés de Santa Cruz, a descendant of the Incas, attempted to bring some sort of order to the country. He was ousted by the whites, who plunged the country into thirty years of anarchy and civil war. In 1879 came the war with Chile, losing Bolivia her only outlet to the sea. At the turn of the century a rich rubber producer provoked an unnecessary war with Brazil, which Brazil naturally won, with the loss of yet more Bolivian territory. Finally in 1932 came a disastrous war with Paraguay which ended with Bolivia's defeat by a smaller but more homogeneous neighbour. Lawyers can happily prove that the war, fought over the ownership of the Gran Chaco, was justified on one side or the other, but as far as the Bolivian soldiers were concerned it was wished on them by an unrepresentative government at the behest of outside commercial and political interests; they wanted no part of it, and only fought because pride precluded flight. Ten thousand Bolivians from the *altiplano* died of tropical diseases before they had even gone into action.

But some constructive effect the war did have. The *indio* other ranks and white junior officers discovered each other as people for the first time. The conscripted *indios* thought of themselves for the first time as Bolivians, as part of a nation, and found themselves considered as such by their white fellow-combatants who had hitherto believed them little better than animals. Also defeat in the war made the younger officers angry, and disposed for the first time to put country above class.

Bolivia at the time, ineptly managed politically by self-satisfied landowners and greedy generals, was economically in the hands of three tin-mining groups, Patiño and Aramayo (both Bolivian), and Hochschild (Argentine). Almost all *indios* who were not scraping a bare subsistence from the soil were working for these millionaires whose profits, like their products, went abroad. It was an explosive situation. The discoveries and disillusionments of the Paraguayan war made sure that it would explode—as it finally did in 1952.

*    *    *    *

Peru had a slightly more cheerful time than Bolivia, but not much. Between 1829 and 1845 she had twelve presidents and the country was in an almost perpetual state of civil war. (On a recent visit to a Peruvian school, I was shown round by the headmaster. In one classroom were pinned up pictures of these presidents, and next to them a natural history series featuring tortoises. The headmaster said dryly, 'A chart of Peruvian evolution. Tortoises, unlike presidents, don't fight each other or rob the treasury.')

This disastrous era for the once-glorious Viceroyalty was ended by the first presidency of Ramón Castilla (1845–51). Castilla was a coastal Peruvian of *indio*, Spanish and Italian descent—a combination which could only happen on the coast. He belatedly proclaimed emancipation of the Negroes from slavery and abolished the head tax on *indios*, which, like slavery, survived intact from the Spanish colonial period. He encouraged education, immigration, railways and telegraphs—matters which his predecessors had neglected in favour of their squabbles. During his second term (1855–62) he promulgated a new constitution which was to last for half a century, though some of his successors took very little notice of it.

Some of his reforms stuck; some didn't. But none of them touched the basic problem of Peru—the feudal system of land tenure which turned the *indios* of the *sierras* into virtual serfs of their Spanish-descended landlords. This same problem of *latifundia* existed, of course, in Chile, but in Peru it was complicated by the fact that the landowners were Spanish-speaking Europeans while their labourers and tenants were Quéchua-speaking *indios*, with a bitter resentment at serfdom in the land which had once been their own. (For years white people believed that the *indios* had forgotten their heritage, but they had not and have not.)

Civil War<br>in Peru

This historic division of Peru, outside the coastal cities, survived into the twentieth century and still survives. In 1924 a group of intellectuals, students, workers and *indios* rebelled against this inequitable society and formed APRA—*Alianza Popular Revolucionaria Americana*—under the leadership of Víctor Raúl Haya de la Torre. Their programme by European standards was moderately socialist; to the Peruvian oligarchy it was red revolution. *Apristas* were harassed, outlawed, victimized, murdered, and on one tragic day in 1936 six thousand of them were massacred among the ruins of the prehistoric city of Chanchán.

*     *     *     *

Ecuador

Peru's neighbour, Ecuador, likes to claim she was the first Latin American country to declare herself free, by her 'cry of independence' in 1809. But her history after independence was no happier than Peru's. As in Peru, government succeeded government without any change in the basic social structure of the country, the only difference being that the dominant part of the country was the *sierra* and that many of the more oppressed people lived on the coast. And, ironically, throughout Ecuadorean history, the most politically responsible group has been not the politicians but the armed forces.

*     *     *     *

Colombia

Colombia had one curious advantage over its two southern neighbours; the original inhabitants, Chibchas and others, had not developed a high enough culture to preserve it, in however bitter and attenuated a form, in the face of Spanish pressure. The native language and customs had largely disappeared, thus saving the country from a strictly racial problem. But all the other problems were there, particularly the purely political ones.

Originally joined with Ecuador and Venezuela (with both of whom it still shares its national colours and its Embassy building in London), Colombia became in succession the Granadine Confederation, the United States of Colombia, and the Republic of Colombia, all this reflecting the usual fight between local and central authority. This was the more natural in Colombia since every region is separated from every other by mountains or jungle, a circumstance which has had two curious results: many provincial cities like Medellín, Cali, and Barranquilla have, unusually in a South American country, achieved almost as much importance as the capital, Bogotá; and for obvious reasons Colombia established the first commercial airline in the Americas, Avianca, in 1919—its only predecessor in the world being the Dutch KLM.

But though Colombia's geographical divisions made in some ways for progress, they also impeded it, since they made it easier for landlords to be big fish in small provincial ponds— though, to be fair, some of them were amiable fish. A potentially ambiguous effect of geography was the comparative political ineffectiveness of the army, potentially ambiguous because Latin American armies, while more often than not believing themselves on the side of the angels, have often been too politically naïve to recognize devils when they see them. In the case of Colombia, military frustration worked well, and for most of the first four decades of the twentieth century Colombia enjoyed constitutional civilian government and a two-party system, the parties being the Liberals and the Conservatives.

But if politically Colombia in the twentieth century resembled Britain in the nineteenth, socially she was more reminiscent of Britain in the eighteenth. The great land-owning families dominated the Liberal Party as well as the Conservative, and the mass of the people lumped together all pure Europeans, all landowners, all the rich, all the Conservatives (even if technically Liberal) as *godos*, or goths. Added to this, Colombia had a disadvantage which eighteenth-century Britain never knew —monoculture. About 80 per cent of Colombia's revenue came, and comes, from coffee, and every citizen's livelihood depended, and depends, on price fluctuations in the New York coffee market.

Small wonder that, in 1948, the murder of Jorge Eliecer Gaitán, a *mestizo* Liberal who had espoused the cause of the

*Social stratification*

masses, touched off a popular revolt which tore Bogotá to pieces and provoked ten years of virtual civil war.

\*     \*     \*     \*

Venezuela: the most misgoverned State?

Next-door Venezuela, like Colombia sitting astride the humpy shoulder of the Andes, vies with Bolivia for the title of the most misgoverned state of modern times. She too had her Liberals and Conservatives, had them indeed throughout the nineteenth century, but their home life was very different from that known in England, and culminated in the brutal dictatorship of Juan Vicente Gómez, known as the Tyrant of the Andes, who almost incredibly ruled the country from 1908 to 1935.

\*     \*     \*     \*

Central America's troubles may seem small compared with those of the huge South American nations, particularly as—for no good reason—Central America is taken less seriously in the outside world. There tends to be a kind of romance attached to Rio, Lima or Santiago, and even—goodness knows why—to that most prosaic of cities, Buenos Aires; but Tegucigalpa provokes only laughter, and the song 'Managua, Nicaragua, is a wonderful town' is, unlike 'Wonderful, wonderful Copenhagen', intended ironically. In the same way, while nobody would regard it as pejorative to describe Argentine as a 'beef republic' or Colombia as a 'coffee republic', for some reason 'banana republic', as applied to Central America, is intended as an insult by the people who gratefully eat the bananas.

Yet Central America has no less respectable a record than anywhere else. While other Latin American nations were arguing about federalism versus centralism, Central America seriously tried, in the Acta de Guatemala in 1821, to form a union of five countries, and even established two years later the United Provinces of Central America. It failed, but they are still trying, and the Central American Common Market looks more hopeful than the more ambitious Latin American Free Trade Area founded in Montevideo in 1961. Central America's troubles too have been no less than those of South America, and have included United States intervention, which no South American country has had to suffer. In a world controlled by power, the Central Americans have inevitably been the poor relations, and their monoculture has not only condemned them to total dependence on an enormous neighbour, the United States, but has made life much easier for home-grown despots.

Despite all this, Costa Rica for one has set the world an example in civilization, while Guatemala has sporadically shown a kind of cheeky gallantry which one cannot but admire. But this belongs to later pages, as does the background of Cuba and Santo Domingo, today so problematical and important, and the development of Mexico which belongs to the next chapter.

# The Mexican Revolution

MEXICO, IN SPITE OF THE FACT that the majority of its people today are Spanish-speaking, differs almost as much from the other Latin American republics as does Brazil. Not only is it the only American country, apart from Peru, to have had a highly-developed indigenous culture before the European conquest; it also pre-dated all the others in having a definitive revolution as early as 1910, whose importance to the American continent is comparable to that of the French Revolution to Europe and the Russian Revolution to the world.

Cortés

When the Spanish *conquistador* Hernán Cortés reached Tenóxtitian, today Mexico City, in 1519, he found there the centre of a civilization at once advanced and barbaric. Its buildings were the equal of anything in the Europe of the time, and the capital itself was cunningly constructed on an island linked by causeways across a lake to the surrounding mainland. The Nahuatl-speaking Aztecs had an accurate calendar based on meticulous astronomical observation, an advanced mathematical system, a form of writing, an efficient army, and a complicated legal and governmental structure.

At the same time their religious beliefs made them capable of barbarities which shocked the most hardened of the *conquistadores*, including as they did a form of human sacrifice which involved tearing the hearts out of living victims—principally prisoners of war. And the Emperor Moctezuma (hispanicized to Montezuma) half-believed Cortés to be a human manifestation of the god Quetzalcoatl, which inhibited military resistance and greatly facilitated the astonishingly rapid Spanish conquest of the warrior Aztec empire.

The consequent demoralization of the Mexicans made it possible to erect over the ruins of the old culture the Viceroyalty of New Spain, which eventually included not only present-day Mexico but the whole of Central America, large sections of what is now the United States, the Spanish Caribbean islands (Puerto Rico, Santo Domingo and Cuba), and, rather improbably, the Philippines. In Mexico itself the proud and ancient Aztec, Mixtec, Zapotec and Maya peoples were either hispanicized or reduced to the level of subservient *indios*. Within a hundred years of the conquest, the native population shrank from an estimated thirteen million to about two million, largely as a result of the importation of European diseases to which the Mexicans had no immunity.

In general, Spanish colonization followed a familiar pattern. The new rulers brought with them the Catholic religion and the institutions of contemporary Spain, more or less adapted to transatlantic conditions. Among its benefits were technological innovations such as the wheel, which the Incas and the Aztecs had not possessed, as well as Spanish domestic animals and European cereals. The Mexicans in their turn gave Europe maize, tomatoes, chocolate (xocolatl is a Nahuatl word) and chicle, today the basis for chewing-gum. On the debit side, apart from the decimation of the population, which has since been more than counteracted, was the usual reduction of the poorer classes to virtual serfdom and the subordination of national interests to those of the metropolitan country.

The Pattern of Colonization

These abuses, coupled with the fresh breezes blowing as a result of the French Revolution and the political changes in Spain, gave rise to the same discontents as they did elsewhere, though they had somewhat different results. In the first place, the *grito de Dolores* of 1810, which is now celebrated as Independence Day, did not arouse the country as the more practical and prosaic municipal protests did in Caracas and Buenos Aires. The very name, 'the cry of pain' has something Mexican about it—though *Dolores*, which means suffering, was in fact the name of a village.

In the second place, the cry was uttered not by an urban crowd but by a rural priest, Father Miguel Hidalgo y Castilla. In the third place—again somehow typical of Mexico, where tragic failure is often more respected than pedestrian success—the protest failed. Father Hidalgo was captured and executed.

But the cry he uttered has rung down the years, and been

echoed by every Mexican who ever fought for social justice. Its immediate results, however, helped no one. The authorities in Mexico City sent a young *criollo* officer, Agustín de Iturbide, to put down the incipient revolt. Instead he declared for independence and had himself named Emperor in 1821. The immediate result was the prompt secession of the Central American provinces. In Mexico itself Agustín I—and last—was overthrown in 1823 and in the following year Mexico became a republic. The early republican years were characterized chiefly by the venality of the almost entirely military Presidents, and, as in the Argentine, by constant strife between supporters of a strong central government and those who favoured a federal system—in this case so loose as to invite anarchy.

External Pressures
Internal troubles were complicated by external pressures. In 1835 English-speaking arrivals from the United States captured a majority of the seats in the legislature of the state of Texas and proceeded to declare an independent republic. (It would be interesting to know whether President Paul Kruger of the Transvaal knew of this when he refused the vote to *uitlanders*.) When the Texan Republic decided to join the United States of America the result was a Mexican–United States war which lost Mexico one-third of its territory. In 1838 the French invaded Mexico to collect debts owed to a French citizen.

These two events were only the beginning of foreign intervention. But in the meantime a group of younger Mexicans had become exasperated both by military humiliation at the hands of outsiders and *caudillismo* at home, epitomized by the name of General Antonio López de Santa Ana. Led by a Zapotec *indio*, Benito Juárez, they were responsible for 'La Reforma', the liberal reform movement which gave rise to the constitution of 1857, and whose main provisions guide Mexico today. It largely owed its ideas to the French Revolution, the comparatively liberal Spanish constitution of 1812, the constitution of the United States, and the views engendered by the liberal European revolutions of 1848.

Its promulgation aroused the instant resistance of Mexican

conservatives, whose reaction coincided with a joint Anglo-Spanish-French invasion of Mexico to collect debts incurred by earlier *caudillo* governments. The British and the Spanish retired on realizing that the Emperor Napoleon III of France was principally engaged in an attempt to add Mexico to the French colonial empire. Napoleon continued to go it alone, drove Juárez out of Mexico City, and with the connivance of the Mexican conservatives placed Archduke Maximilian of Habsburg on the non-existent throne of the non-existent Empire of Mexico.

Maximilian was not up to the job. He disappointed the Mexican conservatives, was deserted by the French, and in 1867 his forces were driven out by the Mexican republicans and he himself was shot, though his charming Empress Carlota was allowed to return to Europe and is highly regarded in retrospect in Mexico today. After this interruption, Juárez was able to resume his presidency, during which he did his best to establish a more egalitarian society.

When he died in 1872 he was succeeded by another *indio*, Porfirio Díaz, who like Juárez came from the State of Oaxaca. In every other way he differed entirely from Juárez. Where Juárez had been what would be today called a socialist, Díaz was a believer in *laissez faire*. Where Juárez believed in trusting the people, Díaz believed in ruling with a harsh hand. His rule delighted foreign investors, and resulted among other things in the building of Mexico's railway network.

But at the same time it made the poor poorer, the rich richer; it restricted access to office to those favoured by the régime; it terrorized the countryside with a police force called the Rurales who seldom arrested suspects but shot them 'while attempting to escape', under the terms of the notorious Fugitive Law—*la Ley Fuga*.

Like all dictators Díaz did not know when he had gone too far. He was hurt and astonished when an enraged populace threw him out in 1910, thus starting the great revolution which has moulded modern Mexico.

**Revolution— by accident**

Like all the great world revolutions the Mexican revolution

started almost by accident and went through many vicissitudes before it hammered out a policy.

Francisco Madero, now enshrined in Mexican history as one of the 'apostles' of revolution, was no Lenin, even less a Karl Marx. He first came to prominence when the dictator Díaz, in an interview with the North American *Pearson's Magazine*, unwisely agreed that Mexico needed an opposition party. The only opposition party existing at the time was led by Madero, and it had unsuccessfully challenged the dictator's power in Coahuila in 1905.

But 1905 in Mexico proved as important eventually as 1905 in Russia. Díaz's remark was regarded locally as an admission of defeat, and in the 1910 elections Díaz was worried enough to jail Madero before the poll. Civil war broke out.

At the beginning the war had little purpose except that of unseating the oligarchy. It was characterized, like most such wars, by quarrels between the various proponents of reform. Frequently it lost its way. Life was not made easier when a dissident revolutionary, Pancho Vila, crossed the border into the United States (admittedly a part of the United States which had formerly been Mexican) and shot up everyone in sight, thus causing a United States invasion.

The United States itself was hardly guiltless of other interference than this. In 1913 the United States Ambassador in Mexico, albeit without State Department authority, had publicly aided a counter-revolutionary attempt by Mexican conservatives, and in 1914 a United States Naval and Marine force shot its way into Vera Cruz on the pretext of preventing German arms being delivered—to the counter-revolutionaries. As if this were not contradictory enough in itself, the United States at the time was supposed to be neutral in World War I.

The first Socialist constitution

The Mexican revolution—fought largely along the railways built under the dictatorship—managed to survive both these gratuitous interventions and the internecine differences among the revolutionary forces. In 1917 the revolution had been successful enough to draw up the country's present constitution. This, though it owed something to the constitution of

1857, broke away entirely from the Victorian *laissez faire* which the earlier charter had accepted as progressive. It re-established the power of the executive, laid down rules for the ownership and exploitation of land, introduced a minimum wage, proposed a social security system, recognized the rights of labour, and definitively drew a line between the rights of the federal government and those of the individual states. It was in effect the first socialist constitution in the American continent and several of its provisions have been followed not only by Latin American countries but by some in Europe as well.

In Mexico itself it was not immediately effective. There were still barrack revolts and political wrangles. But the new pattern had been set. Under President Alvaro Obregón (elected 1921), universal education got under way. Under President Calles a bitter struggle broke out between the Church and the State, much deplored by Catholic writers such as Graham Greene, but which nevertheless led eventually to a more realistic relationship between the two. The old oligarchy was effectively broken, the basic products of the nation (notably oil) were put under national control, and finally in 1940, with the election to the presidency of Manuel Avila Camacho, the period of transition and military predominance was over and the aims of the revolution began to be converted into facts.

In the meantime the various forces which had brought the revolution about coalesced in 1929 into the PNR (*Partido Nacional Revolucionario*). In 1937 the party changed its name to PRM (*Partido de la Revolución Mexicana*). Finally in 1945 it became the PRI (*Partido Revolucionario Institucional*). As the last it has been criticized by democrats as controlling a one-party state, and by left-wingers for being less revolutionary than institutional.

Whatever the validity of these judgements, it is worth mentioning that the PRI has given Mexico a stable and popularly acceptable government for the first time since Hidalgo raised the cry of independence in 1810.

The period between the outbreak of World War I and the end of World War II marked a profound change in Latin America's relations with the outside world, noticeably those with Europe and the United States, though it took some time for the effects to make themselves felt.

Economically, politically, and socially, the years 1914–18 seemed on the surface to leave Latin America virtually untouched. Apart from a few naval engagements it was a static war confined to a limited number of areas in the Old World, and the Latin American attitude was probably best summed up by the Buenos Aires newspaper, *La Prensa*, which for nearly four years led its main foreign page with the same headline, *La Guerra in Europa*: 'The War in Europe'. True, many Latin Americans of European, particularly British, parentage volunteered for the armed forces of the belligerent nations, but they came mostly from non-political middle-class families and their actions had little impact on the countries of their birth.

Yet World War I set going several important processes which were to be accelerated in World War II. The concentration of industry in the main manufacturing nations on the production of war materials naturally affected their ability to supply their Latin American markets. This gave rise both to the small beginnings of local industrialization, and to an increased flow of capital and consumer goods from the United States, which did not declare war until 1917.

Re-orientation of foreign relations

This in turn was responsible for a radical change in Latin America's foreign relations. Hitherto these had been almost entirely with Europe, first with the parent countries, Spain and Portugal, and later with other European countries, notably Britain. Particularly in South America, the greater part of overseas capital investment—railways, tramways, waterworks, gasworks—was British. Textbooks and fashionable clothes were largely French. Military missions, and hence armament purchases, came mostly from France and Germany. At the same time many of the republics sent most of their exports to Europe, and both exports and imports were carried in European ships.

The United States remained, for the South American countries at least, remote. The Mexicans were, not unnaturally, bitterly anti-*gringo*. Central America and the Caribbean countries were occupied off and on by United States Marines, a legacy of the 'Big Stick' policy of President Theodore Roosevelt (1901–08). The Colombians were smarting from the loss of Panama in 1903, when the United States supported a separatist movement and recognized a new republic which would give her a free hand to construct a strategically important canal.

All this had resulted both in increased United States influence and growing Latin resentment in the areas concerned. But further south the pattern had not yet developed. To most South Americans the United States retained the image of the first American nation to cast off European imperialism, while at the same time, being basically Protestant and Anglo-Saxon, it seemed more remote than Mediterranean Europe. French, not North American English, was still the second language of the Latin American upper classes, whose sons went to the Sorbonne rather than to Harvard.

With the war and the impoverishment of Europe, this situation inevitably changed. Trade with the United States increased, and in some countries (e.g. Colombia, Cuba, Guatemala) amounted to 80 per cent or more of both imports and exports. United States ships, often under flags of convenience such as that of Panama, were more and more in evidence in Latin American ports. Inter-American air travel was largely in the hands of Pan-American and Panagra, two associated US firms. Large United States corporations—Standard Oil, United Fruit Company, Braden Copper—dominated huge areas, even entire countries. Along the newly-built highways the cars, trucks and buses were more often than not Fords or Chevrolets; only the now unprofitable trains and the ancient trams were still British, and these, in a period of rising nationalism, were bound sooner or later to be nationalized.

The same growth of nationalistic spirit, common to all the republics, gave rise to increased resentment at United States preponderance. This resentment was reinforced by the great gap between North American and Latin American standards of living; by envy of United States technological superiority; and perhaps above all by a contemptuous or patronizing attitude on the part of many North Americans, which galled people

United
States
influence
grows

who considered themselves as belonging to an older if much less prosperous civilization.

A succession of Republican Presidents in the United States shared this patronizing attitude, in so far as they paid any attention to Latin America at all. Only with the election of Franklin Delano Roosevelt in 1933 did the United States Administration begin seriously to consider its disaffected neighbours. Franklin Roosevelt initiated a so-called Good Neighbor Policy, which while it did little to alter the 'colonial' economic relationship, at least recognized the other twenty republics as partners. Roosevelt himself was widely popular, and even more so was his Vice-President Henry Wallace, later to be forced out of United States politics for his left-wing views.

Consequences
of
World War II

The outbreak of the second world war, though inevitably it further increased United States influence, did no harm to intercontinental relations. Though some Latin American governments, notably that of Argentina, felt some affinity with Germany, the great majority of the people throughout Latin America had no delusions about what Nazism would mean for them, and tended in the more dictatorial and oligarchic nations to equate Hitler with their own home-grown tyrants.

When the United States entered the war in 1941 she flooded Latin America with democratic propaganda, which was naturally understood in a local as much as an international context. From the point of view of the post-war United States, this was to prove something of a boomerang. Roosevelt had died, and his successors Truman and Eisenhower totally lacked his understanding of Latin America. They continued to support dictatorships which were supposedly stable, anti-Communist, and friendly to United States capital, regardless of their domestic misdeeds, and forgetful of the fact that for four years Latin America had been subjected to an unremitting barrage of exhortations to support the cause of freedom. This, at a time when nationalism and social consciousness were growing side by side in almost every Latin American republic, helped to produce the potentially explosive situation which the rest of this book sets out to analyse.

# Part Two

## THE YEARS OF CHANGE

# Social Stirrings

FOR MANY YEARS IT SEEMED as if the Mexican revolution of 1910 had been an isolated phenomenon: it produced no outside effects comparable to those which immediately followed the Cuban Revolution of 1959.

Partly this was due simply to the poor communications of the time: there were no radio sets then in Andean villages: no starry-eyed sympathizers stepped off planes in Caracas or Bogotá. Nor were there the Trades Unions and other organizations to spread the gospel of revolt, and illiteracy and political ignorance were even more widespread than they are today.

Finally, there was no obvious hero, no significant villain, and no apparently clear-cut break with the past as there was in Cuba. Madero was no Castro: he was a politician. His predecessors were no worse than most Latin American rulers of the time, and better than some. And for a long time the Mexican Revolution had no real programme: the Mexicans themselves held confused ideas about the society they were trying to create, even if they were agreed on what they wanted to abolish.

Nevertheless, it would have been strange if there had not been stirrings elsewhere, particularly after the end of World War I, which at least in theory had been fought for democracy, and the success of the Russian Revolution, which in theory had been carried out for the benefit of the dispossessed workers and peasants.

In more sophisticated countries the latter event had immediate results. In Argentina the Communist Party was founded in 1918 (on 6 January, the date when children traditionally receive gifts from the Wise Men of the East). Although its actual power was slight, it terrified the 'oligarchy', and all local discontents were laid at its doorstep. In Chile Communism quickly gained a foothold among the mineworkers. In Brazil a young army officer, Luiz Carlos Prestes, was converted to

*Enter the Communist Party*

Marxism and became a national legend as a kind of Robin Hood of the remote countryside. But outside Brazil, Communism remained a largely urban phenomenon in a predominantly rural society, besides being an alien ideology in a still very parochial continent.

*     *     *     *

It was, not surprisingly, in Peru that the first important native reform movement appeared. The continued existence of 'two nations'—the Europeanized and the *indios*, the coastal and the *serrana*—made Peru as ripe for revolution as Russia had been. At the same time there existed, as there did not in Bolivia or Ecuador, a sizeable middle group who shared the frustration of the masses but had enough education to want to do something about it.

This educated resentment became crystallized in APRA, the *Alianza Popular Revolucionaria Americana*, founded in 1924 by Víctor Raúl Haya de la Torre, a native of the northern provincial city of Trujillo and a graduate of San Marcos University in Lima. Originally, as the name implies, APRA was intended as a continent-wide movement, and its first manifesto was issued by Haya in Mexico City. This somewhat imprecise document underlined the international nature of the movement, its cardinal points being: (1) action against North American imperialism; (2) political union of the Latin American nations; (3) nationalization of landholdings and industry; (4) internationalization of the Panama Canal; (5) solidarity among all oppressed peoples—later amended to a clause calling for the reintegration of the *indio* in national life.

Hope—and disillusionment—in Peru

As late as 1946 I met young Peruvians who were trying to form *Aprista* 'cells' in Colombia and Ecuador, but in fact within a very short time APRA became an almost exclusively Peruvian movement. During the 1920s Peru was ruled by the dictator Augusto Leguía, who characteristically spent large sums on public works but little on education. He was popular with foreign investors, bankers, business-men and landowners, but distinctly unpopular with liberals, intellectuals and the majority of the people, so that he was forced to maintain his position by the usual repressive measures, and Haya had to flee for his life.

APRA however flourished on persecution, and its highly efficient underground organization was able to reach not only the coastal workers but the *indios* of the sierras -the first political force ever to do so in four centuries. Leguía's economic edifice collapsed as a result of the depression in 1930 and he himself died in prison two years later, but this made little change in the political and social structure of the country. Leguía was succeeded almost immediately by the dictatorship of Marshal Benavides (1933–39), and his hand-picked successor Manuel Prado.

But in 1945 the fresh post-war breeze reached Peru, and elections were held which returned the liberal José Bustamante y Rivero, a lawyer and former diplomat, to the presidency. His success was almost entirely due to the support of APRA, thinly disguised under the name of *Partido del Pueblo*, since it was officially outlawed. This should have been the beginning of a new epoch for Peru, but it was not, and this was to a great extent APRA's own fault.

APRA's apologists like to claim that Bustamante only used APRA to get elected and intended to ditch it as soon as he conveniently could, but in fact the *Apristas* proved almost impossible bedfellows. The years of clandestine existence had not conditioned them to coalition. Their mentality was oppositionist, their habits were secretive, their organization and their glorification of Haya's leadership ominously totalitarian. They formed in effect a government within a government, and used threats and intimidation to increase their hold on the country. Many of the younger and more idealistic *Apristas*, including several of my own acquaintances, left the party at this period which should have been one of triumph.

A naval revolt in El Callao in 1948, for which APRA, rightly or wrongly, was blamed, gave Bustamante an excuse to outlaw the party and jail those of its leaders he could catch— Haya escaped the net. But the right-wing and the Army

decided that Bustamante had been too weak and lenient, and less
than a month later came a *coup d'état* which put Brigadier
Manuel Odría in power for the next six years. Though Odría
was no Leguía, it was a decisive defeat for the forces of progress in Peru and if Odría did not actually put the clock back, he
ensured that it could not advance. Haya himself, charged with
'civil crimes', sought sanctuary in the Colombian Embassy,
where he remained for five years, to the great inconvenience
of the neighbours, who had to put up with troops in their
gardens and tanks in their suburban streets. Eventually he
was given a safe-conduct to leave the country.

During this period the name APRA was erased from the
walls it had disfigured and from the pages of Peruvian newspapers, but the mystique survived both this censorship and
the leader's absence. Haya himself, hurrying around Europe
and any Latin American country which allowed him in, seemed
to have mellowed. Loyal *Apristas* claimed that he had learned
the lesson of 1945–48; disillusioned Leftists charged that he had
sold out to the right; rightists alleged that he was still a red,
clothed in convenient respectability.

Which of these assessments was valid will be considered in a
later chapter, but one achievement cannot be denied to APRA:
after four centuries it has awakened Peruvians to the grave
shortcomings of their society.

\*　　\*　　\*　　\*

The first crack in the oligarchic edifice in Peru was a result less
of internal tremors than of the Wall Street crash of 1929.
Across the Andes the same seismic disturbance shook the
rickety structure of Brazilian democracy. The world-prices of
the country's agricultural products, most importantly coffee,
slumped disastrously, resulting in bankruptcy for smaller
producers and unemployment for the workers. In the cities
the nation's emergent industries also suffered, and with the
same consequences.

This economic crisis coincided with a peculiarly Brazilian
occurrence. Power in Brazil has always rested largely with two

of the largest and most populous states, São Paulo and Minas Gerais. By a kind of gentleman's agreement the parties in power have always alternated presidential candidates and federal patronage between Paulistas and Mineiros. In 1930 President Washington Luis Pereira de Souza, a Paulista, broke this rule by backing another Paulista for the Presidency. The disgruntled Mineiros promptly deserted the government party and joined with its opponents in the so-called Aliança Liberal. As candidate for the presidency they chose Dr Getulio Vargas, Governor of the cattle-raising *gaucho* State of Rio Grande do Sul in the extreme south of the country, bordering on Argentina and Uruguay.

He was defeated, but in such a dubious election that few Brazilians believed the published returns, and there was little opposition when the Army, sharing this scepticism, carried out a *coup* and installed Vargas in the palace. He was to remain there for fifteen years and to make a come-back later, and even today, eight years after his death, the influence of his policy and his personality remains.

Outside Brazil, Vargas is often thought of as a kind of transatlantic Mussolini or even a Salazar, but this shows a complete misconception of what he stood for. True, he was in effect a dictator; like Mussolini he promulgated a new constitution based on the corporate state; like Salazar he called it the *Estado Novo*. But to Brazilians he was the first President to represent the little man, and to millions he is affectionately remembered as Getulio. Brazilians, a cheerfully irreverent people, are given to using Christian names, but it is hard to imagine anyone calling the Duce Benito, and even harder to imagine any such liberty being taken with the austere Dr Salazar.

Unlike most Latin American strong men, Vargas did not confine his energies to the construction of showy public works. He tried to diversify Brazil's perilously lop-sided agricultural economy, which had left it at the mercy of the market price of coffee and to a lesser extent of sugar. He gave subsidies to industry and laid the foundations of today's remarkable

*President Vargas of Brazil*

expansion. He spent a lot of money, though not enough, on schooling and sanitation. Above all he recognized the rights of labour, and though his legislation was inevitably paternalistic, he gave the working classes a new sense of their own dignity and power, a factor which can never again be ignored by Brazilian politicians.

Of course, this was part of a world-wide trend which would eventually have affected Brazil whether Vargas had come to power or not, but the fact that authority was on the side of the change saved Brazil, for the time being, from a more violent replacement of the *status quo*. However, Brazil is too vast a country for any man, however wide his powers, to do more than set a process in motion. In most rural areas the feudal relationship between *patrão* and peasant remains and constitutes today the country's most explosive problem. Nor could Vargas do much to control the ever-growing influx into the towns of the impoverished rural workers, and the consequent proliferation of *favelas*—shanty-towns—around the stately but strident cities. To make a really radical attack on these evils he would have had to be more of a dictator or more of a democrat: if he had been the former he could have acted more harshly towards the diehards; if the latter he might have been able to stir the country's social conscience more effectively. Nevertheless when enough time has passed for Vargas to be seen in historical perspective there will probably be a majority of entries on the credit side of his ledger.

**Democratic Elections**

But even the easy-going Brazilians will not for ever put up with one-man rule, however amiably intentioned, and in 1945 Getulio saw the writing on the wall, when army tanks moved menacingly on the palace. He called Presidential and Congressional elections. He could hardly have done otherwise. Brazil, which declared war on the Axis in 1942, was the only South American nation to send its army and air force overseas (to Italy) in the war against dictatorship. The Brazilian navy had also patrolled the South Atlantic. So the democratic triumph had even more immediate repercussions in Brazil than elsewhere.

As soon as elections were announced, political parties, banned under the *Estado Novo*, were hurriedly organized. In favour of the government was the *Partido Social Democrático* (confusingly backed largely by conservatives) whose candidate was General Enrico Gaspar Dutra. Supporting it was Vargas' own more reasonably named *Partido Trabalhista Brasileiro*, or Brazilian Labour Party. The principal opposing party was the more liberal *União Democrática Nacional*, who put up Air Force Brigadier Eduardo Gomes as their candidate. Of the two remaining candidates only one was significant, Yedo Fiuza, who was supported by the Communists.

After fifteen years during which the government had monopolized all the mass media and no oppositionist politicians were known to the public, the results were not surprising. For the presidency: Dutra (PSD), 3,251,507; Gomes (UDN), 2,039,431; Fiuza (fellow-traveller), 569,818; Telles (Independent), 10,001. For Congress: PSD, 26 Senators and 151 Deputies; UDN, 10 Senators and 77 Deputies; PTB (Vargas's party), 2 Senators and 22 Deputies; Communists, 1 Senator and 14 Deputies; Others, 3 Senators and 22 Deputies. Given the circumstances of the election, the most significant result was the number of votes given to the former dictator's personal party, the PTB, and the relatively good showing of the long-outlawed Communists, perhaps partly due to the mystique of their 'Robin Hood' leader, Luiz Carlos Prestes.

Dutra's period in office was marked by considerable horse-trading between the parties, all of them with their eye on Vargas, who was keeping very quiet as a Senator from Rio Grande do Sul. And well they might keep their eyes on him, for these were the results of the 1950 election: Vargas (nominated by PTB and the *Partido Social Progressista*), 3,829,560; Gomes (UDN and two other parties), 2,288,105; Cristiano Monteiro Machado (PSD and five other parties), 1,653,521; João Mangabeira (*Partido Socialista Brasileira*), 9,465.

It was an overwhelming victory for Vargas and possibly a unique case of a former dictator being returned democratically to power at the first possible opportunity. (President Ibáñez del

**Vargas returns**

Campo, a former dictator of Chile, was also re-elected, but only after many years had elapsed.) But it was a purely personal victory for Vargas. His Vice-President, João Café Filho, only scraped home narrowly ahead of the UDN candidate, while in the Chamber of Deputies the PSD had nearly twice as many seats as Vargas' PTB, and in the Senate, more than four times as many.

A coalition was inevitable, but hardly the kind of government Vargas would have wished. Apart from this political handicap, the now ageing President faced other problems. The price of coffee, still, despite diversification, the mainstay of the national economy, dropped disastrously. Industry wilted while Vargas stuck to his policy of 'economic nationalism' and refused to allow foreign investment. The cost of living rose steadily. The Press was critical, Congress was difficult, and the Army was hostile. It was too much for a man accustomed to command, and on 24 August 1954 Getulio Vargas shot himself through the heart and left the nation's troubles to Café Filho. But subsequent administrations, as we shall see, have still had to cope with Vargas' ghost.

\*    \*    \*    \*

Of all the latter-day strong-men of South America, Juan Domingo Perón of Argentina is undoubtedly the best known abroad. To most foreigners he is, or was during his period of power, a flamboyant figure with a spectacular wife, belonging somehow to an earlier epoch. Compared to the drab politicians and hard-faced despots to whom we are accustomed he seems gay, debonair, romantic.

Yet Perón, one must sadly say, was as much a product of the mid-twentieth century as any of his contemporaries. He owed his initial success, and owes his continuing popularity in Argentina, to the same harsh economic and social realities which produced Haya de la Torre and Getulio Vargas.

Argentina in the latter part of the nineteenth century and the earlier years of the twentieth had seemed to be surging far ahead of her neighbours, by evolution rather than revolution.

But in the 1920s the advance slowed down to a crawl. The *Unión Cívica Radical*, having sponsored (though not itself introduced) universal franchise, the secret ballot, and compulsory education, proceeded to rest on its oars and admire the scenery, smug in the certainty that lesser nations were lagging far behind.

The first Radical president, Hipólito Irigoyen, elected in 1916, was an idealistic and agreeable man, with a gift for making spell-binding speeches which to his followers *seemed* to mean something: anyway, he came from the working classes and was thus on their side, and if they couldn't understand what he was talking about that was probably because they weren't clever enough. He was hardly the kind of dynamic leader a crusading party needed, and he was further handicapped by his inexperience of practical politics (he had haughtily refused a portfolio in his non-Radical predecessor's cabinet).

Unable constitutionally to succeed himself in office in 1922, he supported the candidacy of Marcelo T. Alvear, who despite his Radical convictions was a wealthy man of aristocratic background. Alvear was duly elected. But, despite the backing of Irigoyen himself, he did not meet with the approval of many of Irigoyen's supporters, who felt that no one called Alvear could be a proper Radical. The party split, between those who accepted Alvear, and the *Intransigentes* who formed an Irigoyen faction in spite of Irigoyen himself. This division, which still persists today, occupied the party's energies to the detriment of its progressive programme, which became watered down into a kind of vague amiability towards the less-favoured section of the electorate. These were the urban workers and the rural *colonos* and *peones*, the drab descendants of the once-proud *gauchos*, whose day had come to an end with the fencing-in of the land in the late nineteenth century.

In 1928 the Radicals had the sense to reunite for the elections, but at the same time were idiotic enough to put up Hipólito Irigoyen as their candidate. He was elected, of course. The people still loved him, and would anyway have elected a broomstick rather than a Conservative, except in remote rural con-

Idealism—

stituencies where (to quote an Anglo-Argentine colleague), 'when Squire says turn we all turn'.

—and
incompetence

Irigoyen was now an almost senile 77. Always stubborn, he had become more so, and insisted on doing everything himself. Friends who disagreed with him he sacked, and replaced by sycophants who systematically pilfered the public purse, so that when the Crash came in 1929 the Treasury of prosperous Argentina was almost empty. Civil servants' salaries were months in arrears, official letters were not answered, Bills passed by Congress were not signed, and bills presented by creditors were not paid. The Conservatives with some *schadenfreude* said in effect, 'I told you so.' The Radical rank and file became increasingly angry and disillusioned.

The Army, inevitably, stepped in and took control. They had the people with them. It must have seemed to Irigoyen as if the Argentine public were Shakespeare's Roman mob returned to life. Despite the peculations of the sycophants, Irigoyen himself had lived simply, in modest quarters. A crowd invaded his unfashionable home and hurled his few possessions out of the window, including his iron bedstead and his chamber pot. It is an episode of which Argentines are not proud.

The Army suspended the constitution and appointed General José Felix Uriburu, the son of a Conservative President, to the Presidency. In 1932 elections were held, but the Intransigent Radicals were barred from the polls and other Radicals abstained. It was a walk-over for the Conservatives, who were opposed by a coalition candidate of the Progressive Democrats (a party confined to the Province of Santa Fé) and the Socialists (almost entirely confined to the city of Buenos Aires). Another soldier, Agustín P. Justo, was elected President.

He was not a very good President. He failed to eliminate graft, to relieve growing unemployment, or to redress the lack of exports caused by the continuing world depression. In 1937 in a farcical election he imposed his successors: as President, Roberto M. Ortíz, a wealthy lawyer and former Radical; as Vice-President, an elderly, colourless, provincial lawyer called Ramón S. Castillo.

Astonishingly, the hand-picked Ortíz proved a good, honest, progressive and popular President. But he was a sick man. Within three years of his inauguration his sight was failing from a diabetic condition and in 1942 he died. He was succeeded by Castillo, whom I have heard described as 'a cross between Pétain and Neville Chamberlain'. Abroad he succeeded in annoying both the Allies and the Axis. At home, by his pedantic incapacity, he enraged almost everyone.

\*     \*     \*     \*

On 4 June 1943 the Army took over again, amidst almost total public apathy. A garrulous woman rang up my landlady to tell her there was a revolution. 'Good,' said my landlady shortly, and went out shopping. Her reaction was typical—and widely shared. Throughout the day rumours ran round town, and we learned later that President Castillo had fled aboard the destroyer ARA (*Armada de la República Argentina*) *Drummond*, which had politely conveyed him to Uruguay.

*The Army in power*

But life went on. At midday, when we all knew there was no Government, I went to collect a pair of spectacles from Messrs. Lutz Ferrando in fashionable Calle Florida. Standing on the pile carpet of the store I said, 'I didn't know if you'd be open.'

'We *never* close at lunch-time,' replied the smooth asssitant, disdaining such provincialism.

'But there's a revolution on,' I reminded him.

'So I understand, sir,' he replied coldly.

On my way back to the office I saw a policeman telling off a motorist for parking in a forbidden zone. The driver started to reverse and the policeman stopped him again. 'This is a one-way street, sir,' he told him firmly.

'Jesucristo!' exploded the exasperated driver. 'There's a revolution on!'

'That, sir,' said the policeman imperturbably, 'is no business of mine.'

During the afternoon the Army rumbled and clattered into town—entering the business centre the wrong way down a one-way street, under the disapproving eyes of the police. The

65

subways were still running. A few youths decided to jeer and protest, and a few of us went to watch. We were politely discouraged by tear-gas and sought refuge in bars.

There had been only two hold-ups to the well-planned *coup*, which was self-confidently accompanied by newsreel cameras. The Mechanical School of the Navy, on the outskirts of the city, had not been privy to the plot, and gamely opened fire on the advancing Army battalions: four cadets were killed before they were persuaded to desist from futile resistance. And the Chief of Police, a former Army officer, refused to hand over his sword and his headquarters to anyone but a senior officer, who was only found after twenty minutes' search.

Two days later I had occasion to go to the General Post Office, where troops were billeted. Their equipment, tin hats on top, was neatly piled on the marble concourse, and several of them were writing home on picture postcards of the impressive building. I asked one unoccupied soldier: 'What's this revolution about? Fascist? Democratic? Pro-Ally? Pro-Axis?'

He looked at me glumly. 'You ever been in the Army, *ché*? The other day the sergeant came into our barrack-room and told us to get up, see, and put on full kit. Someone said, "What's up, sergeant?" The sergeant said, "You're marching to Buenos Aires, that's what." Well when the sergeant says I'm marching to Buenos Aires I march to Buenos Aires, I don't ask any . . . . silly questions, eh?'

It was the last time that a *coup* in Argentina could be accepted so indifferently, even by private soldiers.

The
Emergence
of Péron

This time the Army decided to run the country itself—and proved quite as inept as the deposed Castillo. Retired lieutenant-colonels were dug out and put in charge of almost everything, radio news bulletins were nicknamed 'Orders of the Day', and telegrams, for no known reason, had to be written in triplicate.

But one lieutenant-colonel was no dug-out. His name was Juan Perón. One of a group of younger officers called GOU (*Grupo de Oficiales Unidos* or *Gobierno, Orden, Unidad*), he was a member of the ruling *junta*. As such he was offered a cabinet

66

post and modestly declined, asking instead to start a new Secretariat of Labour and Welfare. His request granted, he proceeded to build up a powerful Trades Union movement which for the first time included rural workers. Hitherto only a few industries had been unionized, and the Anarchist and Syndicalist unions were weak. In his Welfare capacity he took charge of relief for the earthquake-shattered city of San Juan—though San Juan never saw the millions of pesos collected. In his personal capacity he teamed up with Eva Duarte, a small-time radio and film actress from the wrong side of the tracks who proved an invaluable asset to the bourgeois Perón in winning over the masses in what the rest of the population regarded as appalling speeches in a terrible accent.

Perón was made Vice-President to keep him quiet. It didn't. He was arrested in 1945 by the frightened President, General Edelmiro Farrell. Evita (by now Señora Peron) promptly called out the militant Trades Unionists and marched them on the Casa Rosada. Farrell, more frightened still, brought Perón back and came out on to the balcony to say so. 'We want Perón!' screamed the crowd. 'Why doesn't this damned rabble shut up?' grumbled the General to an aide—inaudible, happily for him, to the people in the plaza, but not to millions of listeners on a nation-wide radio hook-up.

Elections were called. The Radicals, Progressive Democrats, and Socialists formed the *Unión Democrática* with the Communists, which immediately alienated thousands of voters. That was their first mistake. The second was that of the Radicals (who forget nothing and learn nothing). As the majority party they insisted on nominating two party wheel-horses for President and Vice-President. Their names, disastrously, were Tamborini and Mosca—the fly and the tambourine.

The electoral campaign was marked by unparalleled violence and intimidation by the Labour Party (later more realistically renamed the Peronista Party). The *Unión Democrática*'s campaign train was stoned, nearly derailed, and set on fire. When it panted back into Buenos Aires the engine driver sounded the dot-dot-dot-dash of victory on the whistle, and a Communist girl climbed on to a platform gate and made the V-sign.

But victory was Perón's. After the dirtiest campaign, the cleanest possible elections gave him a bare majority of the popular vote, but a concentration on key marginal seats gave him a thundering majority in both Houses of Congress. Smartly, he did not outlaw the opposition, led for most of the time by a Radical called Arturo Frondizi. Instead he bludgeoned the Press into non-existence (*La Prensa*) or powerlessness (*La Nación* and others) by every quasi-legal trick in the book, and when these did not work, the strong-arm boys—literally boys —of the Newsvendors' Union took over. Similar tactics were used with radio stations. Peronista trades unionists brought recalcitrant manufacturers and businessmen to heel (the only strikes condemned were those against the Government by the old-established unions: printers, dockers and railwaymen, the last now nationalized). Women were granted the vote—and pressured into the Peronista Party. Domestics, railway guards, and civil servants were ordered to spy on their colleagues and employers. It was a real dictatorship.

But it was, or masqueraded as, a dictatorship of the proletariat. Regardless of the effect on the nation's economy, wage-rises were granted as soon as asked. New housing projects and workers' centres were started. Hours were reduced. Land, it was announced, would be given to those who worked it. Mass jamborees were held. There were political rallies to which everyone went—particularly as all cinemas, bars and restaurants were simultaneously closed.

The nationalists were catered for too. Regardless of expense the Government ordered transatlantic liners, opened up new overseas air routes, imported expensive military equipment, rewrote school books to teach patriotism instead of history, and printed millions of glossy brochures for backward Bolivians and innocent Europeans about the glory of Argentina.

It was too good to last, and it didn't. The death of Evita in 1953 probably started the decline. She was a working girl, who in her autobiography had stated that when she found there were

68

rich and poor she didn't mind that there were poor but was very angry that there were also rich. A bourgeois army officer could not match that kind of appeal to the less admirable feelings of the masses. Nor did he share his wife's native shrewdness: she had never alienated the Roman Catholic Church; he did. She had, certainly, alienated the Army; but he, surprisingly, alienated it even more. Finally, when in 1955 he was faced with the determined opposition of the Army, the Church, the middle-classes, business and the intelligentsia, he did what Evita would never have done—he fled.

Oddly, his flight did not alienate him from his millions of supporters among the workers. As a later chapter will show, the seeds he sowed are still sprouting. And *Peronismo*, though deplored by every intellectual of the Left and most Trades Unionists abroad, still has its place among the revolutionary movements of Latin America.

# The Post-War Dictatorships

REVOLUTION INEVITABLY ENGENDERS counter-revolution. It is not therefore surprising that in some Latin American countries during the post-war period the forces of reaction should make a counter-attack, and succeed for a time in preserving the *status quo ante*.

What *is* surprising, on the face of it, is that one of these countries should be Colombia, which had prided herself for most of the twentieth century on having internal peace, a democratic two-party system and an army which scrupulously avoided involvement in political affairs.

During the nineteenth century Colombia, admittedly, had shown no more signs of political maturity than most of her neighbours. She suffered the same clashes between federals and centralists, conservatives and liberals, clericals and anti-clericals, as the rest of the continent, and entered the new century in the middle of a civil war. In 1903–04 the country had the humiliation of losing Panama, which became virtually a United States puppet—an injustice recognized by the United States in 1922–26 when it paid Colombia an indemnity of twenty-five million dollars in respect of non-existent Colombian 'installations'.

Conservatives and Liberals in Colombia

In 1910, however, the dominant Conservatives and their Liberal opponents, tired of the constant strife, joined in a brief coalition which drew up a constitutional amendment providing for a guaranteed representation of the minority parties. From then until 1930 the majority remained Conservative. In that year a Conservative split produced another coalition administration under Enrique Olaya Herrera, a Liberal. The 1934 elections returned a Liberal, Alfonso López, to the presidency with a sizeable majority in Congress.

Under López, the Liberals, like the Radicals in Argentina, started well. They pressed ahead with education at primary and secondary levels, enacted labour legislation comparable to that of Vargas in Brazil, and launched a policy of agrarian reform. These last two measures, however, never got further than pious aspirations, and the Liberal dynamic slowed down to a crawl with the election of Eduardo Santos to the presidency.

Santos proved a very gentlemanly Liberal. He came from a 'good' family, owned the sedate Liberal newspaper, *El Tiempo*, and believed in a policy of *convivencia*, or peaceful co-existence which precluded annoying the Conservatives too much. He was more or less a Colombian equivalent of Marcelo Alvear in Argentina, and had much the same effect on the more radical elements of his party as Alvear did on those of the UCR. At the same time he was still much too leftist for the Conservative diehards, and particularly the Roman Catholic hierarchy which in Colombia has long been closer to Madrid than to an increasingly enlightened Rome.

The elections of 1946 brought into evidence the fatal division in the Liberal Party. Their official candidate was Gabriel Turbay, of Syrian descent. The official Conservative candidate was Mariano Ospina Pérez, a rather nice man. It should have been thus a conventional two-party election. But it wasn't.

A former Mayor of Bogotá, Jorge Eliecer Gaitán, felt— not without reasons—that the Liberal Party had become too conservative. Gaitán himself was a *mestizo* of working-class background, and was supported by most of the under-privileged citizens of Colombia. His electoral campaign was hardly a clean one: taking advantage of the foreign parentage of Turbay, Gaitán plastered the walls of Colombia's principal cities with the slogan 'Turco No'. Supporters of Gaitán beat up *Turbayistas* in the streets. The result of all this was that while the two factions of the Liberal Party gained a Congressional majority between them, the Conservative candidate, Ospina Pérez, became President.

This was a disaster for Colombia, however worthy Ospina Pérez was as an individual. No Conservative could at the time have commanded the allegiance of the people. The rich were still embarrassingly rich, the poor uncomfortably poor. Large sections of the country felt that they had been betrayed by the election results. When, on 9 April 1948, Gaitán was assassinated, the working-class *ruana*-wearing citizens of Bogotá, blamed the *godos*—the rich and the conservative—and proceeded to tear the city apart.

It has never been satisfactorily proved where the sympathies of Gaitán's murderer lay; it is generally believed that he was a religious fanatic, but that the Colombian Communists were aware of his proposed action and made their plans accordingly. Some people, with a certain amount of inspired hindsight, have pointed out that the young Fidel Castro was in Colombia at the time, but it seems highly unlikely that he had any serious effect on events.

The *Nueve de Abril*

Be all that as it may, the poorer people of the whole country rose in revolt against the 'Establishment'. In Bogotá itself the Carrera Séptima—the Bond Street of Bogotá—was wrecked from end to end. Government offices were gutted. Cars were overturned and burned. Crowds shouted 'Viva la muerte' and an old woman was seen sitting in the street outside the British Embassy ripping the keys out of a typewriter, one by one.

The female Embassy secretary who saw her thus engaged was subsequently offered escort to her digs by a polite Bogotano gentleman. As he was a Conservative M.P. she declined, and instead walked safely back wearing a red rosette. Foreigners were much involved in what is now called *el Bogotazo*, but such is Colombian hospitality that none were hurt. The Pan-American Union (later the Organization of American States) was meeting in Bogotá at the time, and the Mexican delegation at a crucial moment was having a private meeting in the conference building. They unhooked the Mexican flag from among those of the twenty-one republics, and walked back to their hotel holding it aloft. Both authorities and revolutionaries held their fire to let them pass. An English acquaintance of mine, holding a small Union Jack, was treated with similar courtesy in crossing the road to buy cigarettes.

But the *Nueve de Abril* was not confined to the capital. In the Caribbean port of Barranquilla the hammer and sickle was hoisted on the town hall. In the attractive departmental capital of Cali the local radio announced the formation of the Soviet Socialist Republic of Colombia. All over the country, so-called Liberals and Conservatives, brought up in their political allegiance as Irishmen are brought up to be Protestants or Catholics, began fighting each other, egged on sometimes by priests who should have known better.

Leaders of all parties, including both factions of the Liberals, horrified at the holocaust, formed a coalition to restore peace. They succeeded in doing so among the smoking ruins of Bogotá but failed elsewhere, and for a decade an undeclared and unacknowledged civil war continued in the provinces.

In 1950, with the country still in a state of perturbation and the Liberals once again split, Ospina Pérez was succeeded in the presidency by the extreme rightist Laureano Gómez, a friend of Franco and former supporter of the Axis who had spent many years in Spain. His authoritarian régime was too much for everybody and in 1953, for the first time in half a century Colombia experienced a military revolt. General Gustavo Rojas Pinilla took over.

At first almost everyone—despite a slight feeling of shame at the failure of constitutional government—was relieved. Rojas Pinilla promised an amnesty to those who had taken up arms, freedom of the Press, elections as soon as possible, and above all peace. But within a short time he proved more dictatorial than his legally-elected predecessor—and did no more to redress the centuries-old social wrongs of the country.

In May 1957, a tired, war-worn people, with the support of the army, the business community, university professors, newspapermen and civilian politicians, combined to throw Rojas Pinilla out. In 1958 a Liberal intellectual, Dr Alberto Lleras Camargo, was elected President under an interim agreement by which the Conservative and Liberal parties agreed to a bi-partisan policy, and to vote for each other's candidates at alternative elections.

The Constitution, of course, allowed other candidates to stand and there were grave doubts as to whether the electorate

*Searching for Stability*

73

would prove mature enough at the 1962 elections to resist the temptation to vote for extremists of both factions who chose to ignore the pact.

These fears proved unfounded, and the moderate Conservative Guillermo León Valencia was returned by a healthy majority. Though all was still far from being well with Colombia, it seemed at any rate unlikely that there would ever be a repetition of the *Bogotazo*, and there was enough good will on both sides to preclude the kind of anger and bitterness which produced the Castro revolution in Cuba.

It was still too early, however, for any responsible Colombian politician to risk returning the country to a free-for-all party system until increased prosperity and more widespread education had removed the temptation to seek violent solutions to the people's problems.

\*     \*     \*     \*

Venezuela's post-war troubles came as rather less of a surprise than those of Colombia. As stated in an earlier chapter, Venezuela was during the nineteenth century one of the worst-governed countries in the world, and in the first four decades of the twentieth century she knew nothing remotely resembling democracy, despite the usual legislative and judicial trappings.

From 1821 to 1830 she was a part of Gran Colombia, but when the alliance with Colombia and Ecuador fell apart, she was on her own. At first the country was ruled by a conservative oligarchy, but after ten years sections of the people began to murmur, balancing the evident stability of the régime against its inevitable injustices. However, it would be a great mistake to equate this discontent with anything like a popular movement.

Guzmán
Blanco of
Venezuela

The disgruntled objectors came not from the truly underprivileged (though no doubt they were disgruntled too) but from the same sort of class which had been instrumental in throwing out the Spaniards: the privileged who didn't consider themselves privileged enough. In 1840 they banded together in what they inaccurately named the Liberal Party, and

74

in 1848 they succeeded in overthrowing the Conservative oligarchy. For the next twenty-two years they attempted to rule, but most of the period was occupied by a series of civil wars on the issue of federalism versus centralism—a somewhat artificial question which served to disguise the personal ambitions of the participants. This chaotic situation inevitably resulted in the emergence of a dictator, Antonio Guzmán Blanco, who came to power in 1870. Guzmán Blanco was officially a Liberal, and began by following Liberal principles in everything except tolerating an opposition. Like most Latin Americans of non-Conservative persuasion, he was anti-clerical, and drastically reduced the privileges of the Church. He started a national system of elementary education (though today millions of Venezuelans are still illiterate). He gave government support to the Central University of Caracas (now better known for its political effervescence than its academic activity). He cut import duties and increased the flow of imports, he made war on graft and inefficiency, and—like all effective dictators—he undertook large public works: railways, roads, telegraph lines and seaport facilities.

However, his reforming zeal soon cooled, and he devoted more and more time to consolidating his own power, encouraging his own glorification, and filling his own pockets. When he died in 1888 he left his successors just as many problems as he had inherited, and after a further period of chaos a new dictatorship came into power in 1908, that of Juan Vicente Gómez.

Gómez was a *caudillo* of the old style. The son of a Spanish immigrant and an illiterate *india*, he grew up in Táchira province as a *vaquero*, or cowboy. During his lifetime he fathered innumerable children, and he never had any formal education. He nevertheless looked down on the peasant people from whom he had sprung, believing them too stupid to deserve anything but a dictatorship—a view privately shared by more sophisticated people than he. He did nothing to raise the standard of living which in fact declined, and used the country's growing oil revenue largely to perpetuate his own system and increase his personal fortune. When he died in

December 1935, at the age of 79, he left Venezuela no better off, and no more capable of governing itself, than it had been at the time of independence.

**Democratic ferment**

The widespread relief at the dictator's death was not converted into action by a leaderless population, and a soldier, General Eleazar López Contreras, took over the presidency to avert total collapse. A new constitution was passed by Congress in 1936, and in the same year an advanced labour law was passed, permitting for the first time the formation of trades unions, and providing for such reforms as unemployment insurance and an eight-hour day. To everyone's astonishment the oil workers promptly availed themselves of this law and declared a general strike, 20,000 of them walking out of their jobs.

The government had not intended to be taken all that seriously, and in January 1937 ended the strike by decree, giving the workers a small wage increase. But it was not only oil workers who felt that they could breathe again after Gómez's death. New political parties were springing up. Since elections were indirect and only a minority of the population was enfranchised, the official ACB party (*Agrupación Cívica Bolivariana*) was still predominant in Congress. Despite this, in the 1937 elections, the left-wing opposition, headed by ORVE (*Organización Venezolana*) managed to capture the respectable total of thirty seats.

Frightened by this portent, the government majority decided that all this democracy must be stopped. The 1936 constitution empowered the President to take action against communists and anarchists, but did not define these, so (anticipating a later South African administration) López Contreras declared forty-seven of his political opponents to be communists, and proscribed ORVE and the two other main leftist parties on the same grounds.

**The Politics of oil**

In the economic field he tried to gain popularity by organizing more equitable division of oil revenues, and in 1938 passed a new oil law by which the Venezuelan Government was to get a great share of the oil revenues of the British, Dutch and

United States companies and to use it for the national benefit. The outbreak of World War II however had the effect of reducing Venezuela's oil exports due to the blockade of the Axis powers, the shortage of Allied tankers, and other factors, and the 1938 law brought Venezuela little benefit.

In 1940 elections were held again under the old restrictive, indirect system. ORVE surfaced again under a new name, but promptly split between pro-and anti-communist factions: not that it mattered; the government declared both factions communist anyway, and banned them. However, now for the first time the socialist but anti-communist Rómulo Betancourt appeared publicly on the political stage, as the organizer of *Acción Democrática*, whose candidate for the presidency was the moderate socialist novelist, Rómulo Gallegos. As was only to be expected under the current franchise, only 13 out of the 136 deputies (who chose the President) voted for Gallegos rather than the government candidate, Isaías Medina, but in the circumstances that was as great a portent as the general strike.

Medina's government weathered the oil slump and survived into the boom which began in 1944. A new oil law with the foreign companies was agreed, codifying the entire petroleum legislation for the first time, to the long-term mutual benefit of the companies and the country. In 1944, his newly formed government party won an overwhelming electoral victory by highly dubious methods and looked all set for another four years of rule in the Gómez tradition—and so *ad infinitum*.

But in 1945 several things happened. Medina fell out with López Contreras and the government party split. The end of World War II gave a heart to the democrats, and also forced Medina to terminate the 'State of National Emergency' which he had used to suppress opposition. And the younger, more liberal army officers decided to throw out a régime with no popular support and to back *Acción Democrática*. They approached Rómulo Betancourt.

Understandably, AD was surprised and a little embarrassed by an offer of help from this unexpected quarter. However, the government had by now made any legal opposition impossible, so AD agreed to the officers' suggestion, and on 17 October 1945 the government was overthrown with surprising ease, total casualties throughout the country being only about 2,500. The officers set up an interim civilian government to run the country while a new electoral law was worked out to permit voting by all adult Venezuelans for a constituent assembly.

Other parties besides AD now sprang up, the principal ones being COPEI (*Comitiva para Organización Política y Electoral Independiente*—more simply Christian Democrats); URD (*Unión Republicana Democrática*—left of centre), and the Communists, who had hitherto functioned underground, and subsequently split. At the election in 1946 the AD won a resounding victory with 137 delegates elected, as against 19 for COPEI, 2 for URD, and 2 for the Communists. In the presidential elections next year Rómulo Gallegos was elected President by a large majority over both of his opponents combined, and AD had a similar majority over the three other parties in both houses of Congress.

A Socialist Programme

For the first time in its turbulent history Venezuela had a democratically elected government. It went to work with a will to implement its socialist policy: measures were taken to improve the standard of living; trade unions were encouraged to play a responsible part in affairs; the budget of the Ministry of Health was quadrupled, malaria eradicated, and rural sanitation improved; huge housing projects were undertaken; expenditure on education was trebled; a study was made of means to modernize agriculture and stockbreeding, resulting in a comprehensive plan of agrarian reform.

It all looked too good to last, and it was. Not only were the civilian right-wing becoming increasingly unhappy about all these innovations; but the army was becoming increasingly restive, and many even of the younger officers felt that things had gone too far. On 24 November 1948 these latter gave an ultimatum to Gallegos demanding the exile of Betancourt and the formation of an AD-COPEI coalition. Gallegos said no, and the army seized power once again.

78

# The Post-War Dictatorships

Colonel Marcos Pérez Jiménez became the strong man of the *junta*, and in 1953 under a new and farcical constitution, he was 'elected' President. Venezuela was back under a dictatorship. It was one of the worst tyrannies of modern times.

Tyranny returns

Thousands of political prisoners—members not only of AD but of all the other civilian parties—were imprisoned, tortured, shot, or sent to die in jungle-girt concentration camps. Trades unions were abolished piecemeal until none were left, and labour leaders were treated in the same way as politicians. Schoolteachers were dismissed in hundreds, and the closure of the universities forced students to continue their studies abroad—if they could afford to. A police force called the *Seguridad Nacional* was built up on the model of the Gestapo.

Public works were confined to showy constructions like the sky-scraping *Centro Bolívar* in Caracas, blocks of workers' flats where they could be seen but not where they were most needed, and a hotel on top of a mountain. It is usually enshrouded in mist—and therefore empty. Within a few years Pérez Jiménez had alienated almost everyone except the oil companies and a singularly imperceptive United States government, with whom he was careful to keep on good terms. (The blindness of the Truman and Eisenhower administrations to such dictators as Pérez Jiménez and Rojas Pinilla is responsible for much of the anti-*gringo* feeling in Latin America today.)

But Venezuela had had one brief taste of freedom, and not even the *Seguridad Nacional* could keep Pérez Jiménez in his seat for ever, particularly as the army was beginning to have an uneasy conscience over its part in seating him in the first place. In 1958 a popular revolt, similar to the one the year before in Colombia, threw the dictator out.

A provisional government was formed under Admiral Wolfgang Larrazábal, with the support of the leaders of AD, URD, and COPEI, most of whom had been forced to take refuge abroad. At the elections the same year AD put up Betancourt as presidential candidate, Larrazábal agreed rather reluctantly to stand for the URD, and COPEI's candidate was its founder Rafael Caldera.

In the presidential ballot Betancourt was elected with 49 per cent of the votes, Larrazábal obtaining 35 per cent and Caldera 16 per cent. In Congress AD's showing was not as good as it had been before the dictatorship; it won 32 seats in the Senate and 73 in the Chamber, figures for other parties being URD, 11 and 33; COPEI, 6 and 20; Communists, 2 and 7. In view of this, and of the disastrous effect of democratic disunity heretofore, Betancourt formed a coalition government with the two other major parties.

Like all coalitions this one has had its internal difficulties, but in a more cautious way it has been pushing the reforms initiated in 1945 to 1948. The right-wing is now so discredited as to constitute no real threat, and the army—or most of it—is sufficiently chastened to keep quiet. The threat, indeed, is a different one, and it comes from the outside.

Finding an outlet for reform

Nowhere more than in Venezuela has the mystique of Fidel Castro spread, particularly among the youth who are impatient at Betancourt's comparative caution. The Venezuelan communists, though numerically insignificant, are being fairly successful in embarrassing Betancourt and keeping up the zeal of his youthful critics. There have been several minor unsuccessful *coups*, two of them in 1962 alone. In this, as will be shown later, the Venezuelan government is facing a problem common to many democratic Latin American administrations —how to divert the reforming enthusiasm of the poor and the young into constructive channels, how to persuade them that evolution is preferable to revolution and elections to slogans, and how finally to do it without infringing their democratic liberty.

\*　　　\*　　　\*　　　\*

It is perhaps unfair to include Odría's period of rule in Peru in the same chapter as Pérez Jiménez and Rojas Pinilla. Yet its origins were in a way similar—the reaction of the right to the ebullience and power of the left.

Unlike either Pérez Jiménez or Rojas Pinilla, General Odría did not actually persecute his opponents, though his régime did charge Haya de la Torre with 'civil crimes' as a result of which the latter was penned up for five years in the Colombian Embassy in Lima before he could gain a safe-conduct to go abroad. But, though this was unpleasant for Haya and irritating to the Colombians, there was a kind of good-naturedness which would have been lacking in a really totalitarian state.

In order that Haya should not escape, the tree-lined streets around the Colombian Embassy in the suburb of Miraflores were patrolled by tanks, and residents were stopped and interrogated by soldiers. When a lady resident asked me to dinner the soldier who stopped the car wished her an amiable good evening and asked if I were her fiancé or a revolutionary. She said indignantly that of course I was a revolutionary, and the soldier laughed and waved us on.

Also, unlike the other post-war dictators, Odría voluntarily relinquished his post when his term was up in 1956. (When asked by a United States newspaper correspondent why, he replied with evident feeling, 'I'm tired. Have *you* ever tried to run a country?') It is true he suggested to the electorate that they should support a candidate of his own choice, but they didn't, electing instead a Conservative ex-President, Manuel Prado, and Odría did nothing to upset their choice.

The voters chose Prado neither for his ex-presidency nor for his conservatism, but because he had promised to relegalize APRA, and Haya de la Torre had instructed *Apristas* to vote the Prado ticket. Prado was as good as his word, and APRA was duly legalized. During Prado's term a certain amount was done to redress the imbalance of wealth, power and property in Peru—rather too much to please the Right but not nearly enough to satisfy the Left. The *Plan Peruvia*—whose aim is to industrialize the *sierra*—was proceeded with; a pilot project was set up at Vicos by the Peruvian Government and Cornell University in which the *indios* once again were able to run a village on their own; vital road-building projects, started under Benavides, were continued.

Eighteenth century Hangover

But the greater part of the country still suffered from the hangover of an eighteenth-century economy. Every train that came into Desamparados Station in Lima carried its quota of *serranos*, lugging their humble belongings and looking for a new life in the capital. The new life most of them found was in the slums and shanty-towns, where they settled, to the desperation of both themselves and the authorities, while haughty *limeños* of the upper classes passed by—with honourable exceptions—on the other side.

Prado's term came to an end in June 1962. Elections were duly held. The principal candidates were Víctor Raúl Haya de la Torre, for APRA, Fernando Belaúnde Terry of the *Partido de Acción Popular* (PAP), and General Odría. The final election results, after numerous recounts caused by often frivolous accusations of fraud, were: Haya de la Torre, 557,047; Belaúnde, 544,180; Odría, 480,798. The remaining votes went to the four other candidates, with the result that no candidate gained the one-third of the votes necessary under the Constitution for outright election. In these circumstances Congress must choose between the principal candidates.

In Congress APRA and its allies gained the largest number of seats but not an over-all majority, thus presaging a protracted wrangle. To avoid this the candidates, with the support of President Prado, agreed to come to an agreement among themselves. It might have seemed logical for the two left-wing candidates, Haya and Belaúnde, to come to a *modus vivendi*, but the situation was more complicated than that.

Belaúnde, a relative newcomer to the political scene, had based his appeal to the electorate on two almost contradictory claims. To the Left he insinuated that Haya, after his pact with Prado, had compromised his political purity and sold out to the 'Establishment'. At the same time he played on the fears of the Right by identifying APRA with Communism, a charge which for decades had had no validity but which side-tracked APRA into expending much of its energy during the campaign to dissociating itself from Communism.

Haya therefore came to an accommodation with Odría, the man who had been responsible for his long sojourn in the Colombian Embassy. It is generally believed that under this bizarre agreement Odría would have been given the office of Presidency, to allay the fears of the Right, while APRA would have been allowed to introduce at least the more acceptable parts of its programme.

But none of its programme was acceptable to the armed forces and in July, without waiting for Congress to meet, they staged a *coup d'état* and installed two Army Generals, an Air Force General and an Admiral as 'Joint Presidents'. Their action was certainly largely due to domestic attitudes: the Army in particular had regarded APRA in the same way British units who had served in Kenya or Cyprus might regard Mau-Mau or EOKA.

There were, however, international repercussions, the chief of them being the danger that the *putsch*, following on the ejection of President Frondizi in Argentina, would encourage the Army in other countries to relapse into their old ways. It was significant that among the first Governments to break off relations with Peru were the constitutional but precariously balanced ones of Colombia and Venezuela. Another was that of the United States, which simultaneously cut off all aid under the Alliance for Progress (see Postscript).

It is easy to see the reasons for this United States action, not the least of them being to avoid the old charge of underwriting military dictatorships. But the United States dilemma in Latin America is underlined by the fact that there was criticism of her action anyway: the withdrawal of Alliance for Progress aid, it was pointed out, hurt the very people who had *not* wanted a military take-over—the majority of the electorate and the millions of those disenfranchised by illiteracy.

Whatever the merits of recognizing or not recognizing the new régime, one fact is clear: the *putsch* in Peru was a severe setback to democracy in Latin America, and enabled the *Fidelistas* and the Communists to say quite legitimately: 'We told you so.'

Putting the
clock back

# Caudillismo Unrepentant

SOME LATIN AMERICAN COUNTRIES have been later than others in emerging from nineteenth-century *caudillismo*, and of these the most remarkable is Nicaragua.

A small and relatively little-visited country, it has a good deal in common with some of its better-known neighbours. Its one and a half million people are Spanish-speaking, largely of Spanish and *indio* descent, though there is an English-speaking Negro community along the Caribbean coast. There are few industries and the country lives on the products of the soil. Economically it has always been in the hands of a small minority of landowners, and politically it suffered the same faction fights between so-called Liberals and Conservatives during the nineteenth century. During the earlier part of the twentieth century it was occupied by United States Marines, and the final departure of these in 1932, under Roosevelt's Good Neighbor Policy, marked the beginning of the rule of the Somoza family, which has been in charge ever since.

Nicaragua:
Medieval
Monarchy

President Anastasio ('Tacho') Somoza, always prudently a good friend of the United States, was 'elected' to the Presidency in 1936, and during the next twenty years consolidated both his political and economic power, becoming by far the largest landowner in the country, besides taking a rake-off from all business enterprises. In 1956 he was assassinated, but his removal made little difference.

His eldest son Luís was First Designate, or Vice President, and quite constitutionally took control—the constitution had been framed by his father. His second son, Anastasio Somoza junior, or 'Tachito', a graduate of West Point, remained firmly in charge of the National Guard, a body which efficiently combines the functions of Army, Police Force and political shock troops. Somoza was dead: long live the Somozas.

Naturally there were Nicaraguans who resented their country being run by what amounted to a medieval monarchy, and there have been several attempts to depose the family. One of these was in June 1959, when it was announced that an invasion by exiles and mercenaries had been launched from Costa Rica. The Nicaraguan government reported that this was being smashed on all fronts, so I went to find out what was actually happening.

At the time the Nicaraguan Embassy and Consulate in London did not figure in the telephone book, there was no Ambassador, and the country's affairs were looked after by a British-naturalized Austrian, who was indignant at being telephoned. A more amenable official suggested I get my visa in Havana, Cuba. There the Embassy was in the phone book, but with the wrong number, and the Consul, when finally located, proved to be a harassed little man working for a North American paint company, who provided me with a multiplicity of documents and forgot to charge the fee. He didn't know what was happening in Nicaragua.

At Las Mercedes airport in Nicaragua an immigration official looked at a Chinese Nationalist passport upside down and asked the bearer if he were German. The customs officer glanced through all my books and papers and held up everyone while he finished a funny story by Paul Jennings. On the road to the capital, Managua, the National Guard twice held up the taxi in the dark but waved us on when the driver said he came from the airport.

As I unpacked in my ground floor room in the old-fashioned hotel built round a *patio*, a skinny arm came through the window and a woman's voice begged, 'Alms for the love of God, sir.' A 10 p.m. curfew had been imposed, so before it fell I took a walk along the quiet, tree-shaded streets between the one- and two-storied Spanish-style houses. People were sitting on the pavements outside their open doors, in rocking-chairs, gossiping and laughing quietly, to the accompaniment of muffled radios indoors.

The
Unnoticed
Revolution

Back at the hotel I asked, 'What about this revolution?' Everyone shrugged. There was a strike. It was said there was an invasion. It would be a good thing if there were a revolution, of course. Somoza was a dictator and a thief, like his father before him. This freedom of speech was, and is, general, because unstoppable: everyone is against the government except those who work for it. But there is no freedom of anything else, and the single, Somoza-owned TV channel devotes most of its time rather irrelevantly to anti-communist films provided by the United States Information Service.

I called on Don César Vivas, assistant editor of the solitary survivor of the free Press, *La Noticia*, independent liberal. I found him in the newsroom, open to the street on the edge of Managua's teeming market. Like most people he was against the government, admired Fidel Castro and liked the democratic Ticos (Costa Ricans), but he wasn't allowed to say so. 'I'm afraid the paper is very dull,' he apologized. He took me up to his home town, Masaya, twenty-five minutes by bus through rolling tobacco country, a sleepy little place on the slopes of a volcano. He pointed to a fortress on top of a mountain. 'We had a battle there with the Yanquis in 1912,' he said. I asked who had won. 'Yanquis. Twice as many men and far better equipped. But we killed a lot of them.'

In Masaya a gushing young woman with dyed auburn hair, who professed herself 'just crazy about comparative religions', showed Vivas some poems she had written and he said he would print three. 'They aren't very good,' he confided to me, 'but it will be nice to print something the censor can't cut out.'

Back in Managua that evening we took a Volkswagen taxi to the house of a Palestinian Arab who was entertaining several people including a National Liberal Senator, and sat in rocking-chairs and talked over iced scotch and sodas. For half an hour the conversation raged in an argument about Israel, but then it veered homewards and everyone turned on the Senator, a dignified, grey-haired man in white trousers and an open-necked shirt. 'But,' he expostulated, 'if this were a dictatorship as you all say, you couldn't talk like this.'

'I can talk like this,' said Vivas, 'but can I print it?'

'We are in a state of war,' said the Senator sententiously, and everyone laughed.

# Caudillismo Unrepentant

In San José, Costa Rica, I called on Dr Lacayo Farfán, the leader of the Nicaraguan rebels. A Costa Rican Congressman —oppositionist and anti-*yanqui*—had just declared that, 'In Nicaragua it is not simply a fight against a dictatorial régime; it is a fight against the United States.'

'We are not fighting the United States,' Dr Lacayo told me. 'We are only fighting to destroy a dictatorship of twenty-five years' standing. But at the same time we believe that United States policy has served to help dictatorships with money and arms. However, we believe that in the very near future the United States will change that policy for one of better relations with the emergent democracies. In Latin America we must try to have free governments and not dictatorships supported by armies, whose equipment and armament are sent by the United States supposedly for continental defence but which in fact are used against the people. The United States will have to be more careful to whom it sends arms.

United
States
involvement

'The people of Nicaragua intend to continue fighting in every way to destroy a government which is an affront to democracy in Latin America. We may have temporary setbacks, as is to be expected in any revolution. But that does not mean that the fight is over. We expect success because all Nicaraguans are determined to have in Nicaragua a free government which will be an expression of the citizenry's will.'

I suggested that he was perhaps rather optimistic with his few hundred men at most against the well-equipped and highly disciplined 5,000 men of the National Guard, and that while it was true I had found the Nicaraguans almost 100 per cent against the government, they didn't seem inclined to do anything about it.

'That will come,' he said. 'Time is our ally. The current of history is running against the dictators and the Nicaraguan people will not be left out.'

In the event, the revolution failed and Luís Somoza felt confident enough to give the captured rebels a somewhat derisive talking to and to set them free. But more than time is now against the Somozas: the mystique of *Fidelismo* had already

87

penetrated Nicaragua in 1959; it has been more widely dif-
fused now. And, while Dr Lacayo's revolution failed largely
because it was basically supported only by the middle class, any
subsequent disturbance is liable to be a good deal more widely
based—and a good deal less gentlemanly.

*     *     *     *

If, even to the Nicaraguans, the Somoza dictatorship seems to
have an almost comic-opera character, the recently overthrown rule of Rafael Trujillo in the Dominican Republic had
nothing of the kind.

Trujillo and the cult of personality

Generalissimo Rafael Leonidas Trujillo Molina, *El Benefactor* and Father of the New Nation, ruled the Republic for
thirty-one years from 1930 to 1961, though he occasionally
allowed friends and relations to occupy the actual post of
Presidency. Until his assassination it was impossible to escape
the imprint of his ubiquitous personality.

The country's capital, Santo Domingo, the oldest European
city in the New World, was renamed Ciudad Trujillo in his
honour. True, as Mayor he had been responsible for its reconstruction after an earthquake, but no one suggested renaming
Warsaw when it was rebuilt after the war. Streets, schools,
hotels, suburbs were named after the dictator; his picture
hung in every office, hotel bedroom, bar, restaurant and public
building; his bust adorned every lobby; bookshops abounded
with fulsome biographies in Spanish and English; the principal newspaper, *El Caribe*, featured his picture on the front
page—and usually on other pages too—in every issue. It was a
cult of personality which might have made even Stalin blush.

Like most such régimes, that of Trujillo was ultimately
dependent on fear—but it was not only fear of the dictator, but
also of a possibly anarchic alternative. Santo Domingo, as the
country first called itself, declared its independence from Spain
in 1821, but in the following year was occupied by the neighbouring Negro republic of Haiti who ruled inefficiently until
1844. Independence was once again declared, and a period of
chaos was followed by Spanish reoccupation in 1861, which

lasted until 1865. A third revolt finally removed the Spaniards, but their influence was soon replaced by that of the United States. Never having been permitted to govern themselves, the Dominicans not unnaturally proved ill-fitted to do so, and for a large part of the twentieth century the country was occupied by United States Marines. The occupation effectively precluded any experience in self-rule, and in the long run exacerbated the ills which in part had brought it about. It was a vicious circle, and the republic seemed doomed to a permanent cycle of chaos and foreign domination.

In these circumstances it was not surprising that the people welcomed the strong hand of General Trujillo—himself trained, incidentally, by the United States Marines. A senior official of the Dominican Ministry of Education, whom I met on a seminar in Jamaica in the early 1950s, put it to me like this: 'I don't approve of dictatorship any more than you do. But I remember in my childhood being taken out of the house at night and hidden because of civil war. My predecessors in office never knew where or when the money was coming from to pay the teachers, let alone themselves. They had no security of tenure—a violent change of government could lose them their job tomorrow. Do you wonder that I put up with Trujillo?'

And, of course, in his thirty-one years of rule Trujillo did, physically speaking, transform the country. Out of poverty, illiteracy and chaos he brought comparative prosperity, widespread (if mostly elementary) education, and almost Germanic order. Ciudad Trujillo was one of the neatest and cleanest (and dullest) cities in the hemisphere. In contrast to neighbouring Haiti, Dominicans enjoyed telephones that worked, a good highway system (peppered with road blocks and military posts), rural schools, handsome public buildings, and new housing estates with large billboards reading 'Obra de Trujillo'. (One resident of such an estate painted gratefully on his house: 'My faith is in God and in Trujillo.')

But for a new generation which no longer remembered the chaos of former times all this was not enough to make up for

'The
Benefactor'

the total lack of all freedom: unlike the Nicaraguans the Dominicans could not even talk; the only criticism of the Benefactor I ever heard in a public place was from an intellectual so despairingly drunk that he was virtually incomprehensible, which was probably just as well for him.

At the same time criticism from abroad was becoming ever stronger. The Generalissimo was tactless enough, despite his drum-beating anti-communism, to anger the United States, and in 1960 a palace official said to me wryly, 'We are the only country in the world which is regularly attacked by both *Pravda* and the *New York Times*: all we need now is for Field Marshal Montgomery to announce that the Benefactor is a fine chap.' Another official admitted candidly, 'The stream of history is against us. I think the Old Man's policy has been basically right; even if the cult of personality has been carried too far, this country owes him everything. But we'll be pushed out.'

Inside the country the predictable hostility of students, intellectuals and businessmen was reinforced by the only non-official voice which could not be completely muffled, that of the Catholic Church, which began demanding less homage to Caesar and more to God. An abortive invasion by exiles from Cuba in 1959 had increased the jitters of the government, and it was followed the next year by the discovery of an inept right-wing plot to assassinate the Generalissimo.

Thus beset on all sides Trujillo decided to insure against the future. On 27 April 1960 his government issued a sweeping decree, legalizing the Communists and the Jehovah's Witnesses (to annoy the Church), calling elections for 1962, and ordering an opposition to be ready (a senior minister, Don Manuel de Moya, told me optimistically, 'Atatürk did the same thing.').

Assassination

But it was too late. On 31 May 1961, the General's car was ambushed and he was shot to death. Radio Caribe announced that 'The Benefactor and Father of the Nation' had 'fallen victim to a treacherous attack' and the shaken government ordered nine days of national mourning.

This was the day for which all Dominicans had hoped and feared. Would there be chaos? Would there be Castroism?

Would there, perhaps, be freedom? In the event the change was not so swift as most would have predicted. The puppet President, Joaquín Belaguer, remained officially in office. The Organization of American States sent a Commission to find out what was going on. Trujillo's innumerable relatives began moving circumspectly out of the country. A military and civil *junta* was set up to 'assist' the President. Political parties began to spring up. Foreseeably, citizens started to demonstrate in the streets—a luxury they had not enjoyed for a generation. There were plots and arrests and in January 1962 the President, tainted with *Trujillismo*, was replaced by a liberal intellectual, Dr Rafael Bonnelly.

It is too soon as yet to say whether the present interim régime can steer the country peaceably towards a solution acceptable to the majority of its citizens. But at least the Benefactor's death has not resulted, as many feared, either in total disruption or in a dictatorial *coup* from the Left or Right. Conscious of the proximity and power of both Cuba and the United States, the extremists have walked warily, and responsible Dominicans may be given the time and opportunity to lead their country at long last towards a system of government by popular consent.

# The Bolivian Revolution

IT IS FAIRLY GENERALLY ASSUMED that the Cuban Revolution of 1959 constituted the first real social and political upheaval in Latin America in modern times, or at any rate that it was the most important event since Mexico broke with the past in 1910. This is understandable because of the close involvement of both the United States and the Soviet Union in Cuba, which thus became involved in the Cold War and attracted a degree of outside attention it would not have done otherwise.

Nevertheless the Bolivian Revolution of 1952 antedated Castro's triumph by nearly seven years. Due to Bolivia's comparative geographical isolation, the lesser involvement of the great powers, and the lack of a picturesque leader, this earlier event has been largely overlooked. But it stemmed from even deeper roots of frustration, and may in the long run have as important an effect on continental history and social development as the victory of the *barbudos* in Cuba.

War: catalyst of change — The basic causes of the Bolivian outbreak have been outlined already. They culminated in the disastrous and futile Paraguayan War of 1932–35, in which the German General Hans Kundt led the Bolivian forces to defeat. Among the side effects of this war were a new awareness among the *indios*, a sense of disillusion among junior officers, a new sympathy and understanding between both these sections of the population, and a widespread weariness and disgust at the generals and politicians who had been running the country so ineptly and inequitably for the previous hundred years.

This dissatisfaction found expression in 1940 with the foundation of the MNR—*Movimiento Nacionalista Revolucionario*—a curious amalgam of malcontents. Headed by Dr Víctor Paz Estenssoro, former Professor of Economics at the University of San Andrés in La Paz, it was originally an alliance between liberal intellectuals and the dissatisfied young officers.

92

Later it absorbed other elements with nothing in common except objection to the *status quo*, notably the remnants of a fragmented Marxist group the PIR—*Partido Izquierdista Revolucionario*—and the organized tin-mine workers under Juan Lechín, a somewhat rabble-rousing figure of whom more was to be heard.

In 1943 the government of Enrique Peñaranda broke off relations with the Axis powers. This fortuitously created an impression abroad that all subsequent events in Bolivia were connected with World War II, which in fact to most Bolivians was a remote issue. Almost immediately after the rupture, Peñaranda was deposed by a *coup* carried out by a 'lodge' of army officers organized on the lines of the 'lodge' which carried out the *coup* of 4 June the same year in Argentina and unintentionally paved the way for Perón.

Peñaranda was replaced by Major Gualberto Villaroel who shrewdly took several MNR members into his Cabinet and named Paz Estenssoro as his Minister of Finance. Due to the factors mentioned above, however, the United States interpreted the *coup* as a machination of the Nazis and the Argentines (the latter being regarded widely at the time as pro-Axis) and refused to recognize the new government. Its example was followed by the docile governments of all the Latin American republics except Argentina, which at that time for largely internal reasons was going through a bitterly anti-*yanqui* phase.

Villaroel, finding this isolation unbearable, eventually dropped the MNR from his Cabinet, and Paz Estenssoro sought refuge in Argentina. His choice was probably dictated largely by convenience, but apparently to Washington it was proof that he and the MNR were the real pro-Nazi flies in the Bolivian ointment, and the United States recognized Villaroel's rump government. It was followed by the other republics.

The Allied victory in 1945—which it must be remembered included the massive Soviet advance on the Eastern front—brought stirrings among the masses in Bolivia as it did elsewhere in the American continent. Despite belated United States recognition, Villaroel was now identified in the public

Fascism discredited

93

mind with a discredited Fascism, as well as with the reactionary local régimes which had preceded his. In July 1946 disorders broke out in La Paz at the end of which a mob invaded the Presidential Palace in the Plaza Murillo, dragged out Villaroel and several members of his Cabinet, and hanged them from lamp-posts around the square. Although, as always in 'popular' insurrections, only a small part of the population was involved in the violence, any *Paceño* today can point to a particular lamp-post and say, 'Minister of so-and-so.' It was a traumatic experience, even for Bolivia.

To the great majority of the people, Paz Estenssoro (no Castro but a conventional-looking, pipe-smoking economist) remained the figurehead of their discontent, and his popularity was increased by what was considered Villaroel's scurvy treatment of him. But he remained in exile in Argentina: the revolutionary force had expended itself in the La Paz riots, the shock of the mass hangings had proved too much for many oppositionists to swallow, and the Right wing continued to govern. In fact so secure in their position did the reactionary forces feel that in May 1951 the government of Mamerto Urriolagoitia (a Basque surname which most Bolivians couldn't pronounce) felt able to call elections. They were after all protected by a constitution in which the vote was restricted to literate males, a small percentage of the population, and probably thought too that the success of the official candidate, Gabriel Gosálves, would be assured by the political differences which split the Left.

They were in for a shock. Despite a restricted franchise which favoured the well-to-do and the *status quo*, Víctor Paz Estenssoro, although absent, won 45 per cent of the 120,000 votes for the presidency, while the MNR, though not in the majority, made an impressive showing in both Houses of Congress. But, though Paz Estenssoro had considerably more votes than Gosálves, he did not have the absolute majority which would have automatically returned him to the presidency. Without this it was up to Congress, with the MNR in the minority, to choose between the competing candidates.

This constitutional provision (similar to the one in Peru, though this only demands one-third of the total vote) was originally designed to ensure a fair balance between the Executive and the Legislature and to put a curb on potential dictators. In fact it has in both countries caused nothing but trouble, as it did in this case. The probability was that Congress would have chosen the official candidate, which would have provoked massive MNR resistance and possibly civil war. We shall never know, because it was a risk the army was not prepared to take, and on 16 May, before Congress had voted, Urriolagoitia resigned and went prudently to Chile, handing over the reins of government to a military *junta*.

The *junta*'s first action was to outlaw the MNR on the grounds that it was a dangerous alliance of Nazis and communists, and that it was intending to nationalize the mines (which it was) and to institute a dictatorship and a reign of terror (which it wasn't). The negative action of proscribing MNR was however almost the only thing the *junta* could agree on, and in April 1952 its fragile unity was broken when one of its members, a General Seleme, defected to the MNR.

Following this the mineworkers rose, availing themselves of the dynamite used in their work to blow up railways and barracks and capture military equipment. In La Paz itself the urban proletariat took to the streets and public utilities were blown up. The army, though it did not defect to the rebels, did not fight them very hard; the junior officers were still sympathetic towards their less fortunate fellow citizens, while the rank and file was composed of these same citizens. Only the Military Academy held out against great odds long after the issue was decided, until the woman head of the Red Cross went under a flag of truce to persuade them that their gallantry was useless.

By 11 May it was all over bar some sporadic shooting. For the first time in the history of Latin America the impassive citizenry of a South American country had decisively defeated the armed forces of the nation.

But it was not the entire citizenry which had risen, even now. The Indian *campesinos* had remained suspiciously aloof.

*A Military Junta*

Victory for the citizenry

Even in La Paz, while fighting was still going on, I saw little bowler-hatted Indian women, in shawls and multitudinous skirts, with burdens on their backs, plodding about their business as if the bullets flying around them had nothing to do with them.

Perhaps, indeed, Bolivia's violent history has made the whole population somewhat *blasé* about violence and death. The day the shooting stopped, when fire-hoses were still playing on burning buildings, a queue was waiting outside a cinema to see a foreign feature film called *Blood in the Streets*, and while the battle was at its height some friends of mine had to coax their maid to take shelter instead of standing at the garden gate to watch. The newspapers impartially published pictures and obituaries of socially prominent people killed on both sides ('For his country,' in the case of the rebels, 'Doing his duty,' in the case of the others) and their friends and relatives condoled with each other on the terrace of the Sucre Palace Hotel.

Be that as it may, the *campesinos* took virtually no part in hostilities: they had seen so much bloodshed and none of it had bettered their lot. In the closing stages of the fighting a rumour went around La Paz to the effect that the *campesinos* were marching on the city, but it was put about by the rebels to demoralize the government, and if any *campesinos* marched they certainly did not arrive.

Problems of Government

This suspicion and indifference was something the government had to overcome, if it claimed to be representative of the people as a whole or to have peasant support in the event of Right-wing counter-revolution. But, though the *campesinos'* suspicions were genuine, their indifference was largely feigned —in four centuries of oppression they had become remarkably good at feigning.

As early as 1936, at the end of the Chaco War, the *campesinos* of the province of Cliza, in the department of Cochabamba, had started a *sindicato*, an agrarian co-operative group, to lease the land they worked, thus becoming tenant farmers and freeing themselves from the obligation of rendering unpaid services to the *patrón*. The landowners banded together to outwit this

96

scheme by legal quibbles, and expelled the *campesinos* from the land they had lived on all their lives. This apparent tactical defeat was a strategic victory for the *campesinos*, for in the climate obtaining after the Chaco War, the news of it quickly spread among the *indios* of the country. These recognized it as the beginning of a battle which was not localized but which involved all the *campesinos* in the country.

In 1947 the suppressed *sindicato* was reborn, and a Quéchua-speaking PIR member, José Rivas (long exiled in Argentina so that his claim to speak no Spanish is to be doubted), became its head. In 1949 the MNR began wooing the peasantry, though their advances were ignored by Rivas who distrusted their more moderate approach. Nevertheless, between them Rivas and the MNR began to awaken the political conscious-ness of the peasants, though the ideological differences be-tween them were to have subsequent divisive effects.

Meanwhile, apart from the difficulty of organizing the *cam-pesinos*, the MNR government had other troubles. Among other things it was under the obligation of fulfilling its pledges to function democratically, which meant allowing a certain free-dom of action and speech to enemies who would have had no hesitation in overthrowing it undemocratically.

By now the Right was so discredited that it would have had no chance of achieving this object: the landlords who were ex-propriated in the first years of the revolution could not pos-sibly return because the *campesinos* of whatever faction would not have allowed them to. The big tin-mining groups, Ara-mayo, Patiño and Hochschild, had been compensated (largely to placate United States governmental opinion) and in any case had so much money salted abroad that they had no need to bother themselves any more about troublesome Bolivian politics.

The Left, on the other hand, could still wreck the revolu-tionary government. Juán Lechín's tin-miners felt themselves the authors of the revolution, and tended to believe that the nationalization of the tin mines was supposed to benefit the miners rather than the country as a whole. They demanded

National-
ization

97

higher wages and shorter hours and indulged in capricious absenteeism, so that Bolivian tin was soon costing a good deal more than the world market price. At the same time they insulted and threatened foreign managers and technicians, who left in large numbers as a consequence, thus further decreasing the efficiency of the Bolivian mines.

The nationalization of the railways also proved disastrous from the short-term point of view. The most important of these lines, necessary for taking the tin out and bringing much-needed new mining machinery in, was the Bolivian end of the British-built and owned Antofagasta (Chile) and Bolivia Railway. In 1961, nine years after the revolution, this was in as parlous a condition as the mines; the tracks were in a dangerous condition, and of sixty main-line locomotives only eighteen were still in working order. In 1962 the Bolivian government swallowed its ideological principles and asked the British back again—to the amusement of sections of the British Press who felt that Great Britain was no good at running nationalized railways either.

Despite these troubles and setbacks the Bolivian government pressed ahead. Paz Estenssoro governed under his 1951 mandate until 1956 when elections were held for the first time under universal suffrage, returning the MNR and Dr Hernán Siles Zuazo to office. At subsequent elections in 1960 MNR again triumphed, and Dr Paz Estenssoro came in for a second term. Government teams went to mining centres such as Oruro to persuade the miners it was in their own interests to work properly. Other groups went to persuade the *campesinos* not to hold back the progress of the country (as had happened in Haiti) by fragmenting into *minifundia*, or subsistence small-holdings, but to band together into co-operatives or collectives. The division between these last is traceable to the original differences between PIR and MNR, but the government seems so far to be succeeding in keeping both functioning without undue strife—at farms of both kinds which I have visited the Quéchua- and Aymara-speaking workers showed a gaiety and enthusiasm which was formerly entirely lacking among a hitherto dour people. Finally the government has initiated an impressive—and necessary—programme against illiteracy.

Unfortunately the MNR itself is not without its internal differences. Though this is not acknowledged, it is split into two factions, the so-called *Socialistas*, middle-of-the-road and mostly intellectual, personified by Paz Estenssoro, and the *Izquierdistas*, or Leftists, personified by Juán Lechín, well to the left of Centre and to some extent Trotskyist. The *Izquierdistas* are divided into four different groups, including the communists. These last, however, are not strong in Bolivia any more than are the *Fidelistas*, and for the same reason—both are of foreign origin, and the Nationalist element in the revolution, as MNR's title implies, was a strong one.

The successes and failures of the régime as well as its internal stresses, bear a considerable resemblance to the situation in Cuba, with one important difference: while Cuba has earned the implacable hostility of the United States and the friendship of the Soviet bloc, Bolivia since the revolution has gained massive North American support. Between 1953 and 1959 Bolivia received in aid and loans from the United States a total of $24,000,000, not counting 'invisible' assistance channelled through United Nations agencies—a far higher *per capita* amount than that given over the same period to any other Latin American country. On top of this is the so-called *Operación Triángulo* for Bolivian development, in which the participants are the United States government, the German Federal Republic and the Inter-American Development Bank (BID).

*United States Aid*

Cynics suggest that the reason for this United States amiability towards a left-wing revolution is that while the principal capitalist investors in Cuba were United States citizens, the Bolivian tin mine owners were not. This may indeed be part of the truth, but it is not the whole truth. During the Truman and Eisenhower régimes the State Department seems to have acted often with little guidance from above in all but Cold War questions, and even its separate departments appear to have to some extent pursued independent policies. Certainly, the department which was responsible for Bolivia seems to have been quick to realize the fact behind President Kennedy's subsequent sponsorship of the *Alianza para Progreso*—that no Latin American government could long survive which had not the final support of the people, meaning in fact a reformist and leftish régime. Where such régimes were not communist it was obviously politic to support them before they became so in default of other encouragement. (There are undoubtedly more idealistic motives behind this policy, but they are not the ones which on the whole commend themselves to United States legislatures).

Free
enterprise
supports
Socialism

Such assistance can of course be an embarrassment to the recipient government in that it can be accused—as the Bolivian government *has* been accused—of being in the pay of the *yanquis*. This aid must therefore be generous enough, and well-distributed enough, to ensure that the revolution is successful and therefore popular. One is thus faced with the paradoxical situation that the free enterprise United States, in order to preserve the friendship of its southern neighbours and its own security, must in Latin America support socialistic régimes.

But whatever the United States does or does not do, the Bolivian revolution was the achievement of the Bolivians themselves, and the clock cannot be turned back. In particular the country's huge Indian majority (out of three and a half million people they form perhaps 80 per cent) has emerged from four centuries of sullen silence and been transformed in a decade.

Here is a small but significant piece of evidence. Before 1952 Indians, even in La Paz, scarcely ever spoke to strange Whites except when addressed; then they usually stared or giggled, and anyway pretended ignorance of Spanish. In 1961 I was caught in a rainstorm in one of the steep, narrow streets of La Paz and sheltered in a doorway with four Indian women. They were dressed, as before the revolution, in national costume, but their bowler hats, blouses and skirts were brightly coloured instead of black, and they had on nylons and neat shoes.

They were speaking Quéchua but politely switched to

Spanish for my benefit, and one of them said to me, 'Dreadful weather, isn't it?'

I told her that where I came from the weather was often like that.

'Oh,' she said. 'Where do you come from?' 'England,' I told her. 'What's England like?' she asked. 'Greener than here because we have even more rain.'

Another woman, showing the usual South American preoccupation with population statistics (not surprising in a continent with the highest birth-rate in the world) asked, 'How big is it, and how many people are there?'

'Much smaller than here,' I told her. 'But we have fifty million people.' Seeing them a little lost, I added, 'About six times as many as you.'

There was a gasp of astonishment and a third woman asked, 'But how can you feed them all?' 'We can't,' I explained. 'We have to sell other things to buy food.' After a thoughtful pause the first *india* said, 'Just like us.'

I told this story to President Paz Estenssoro. He took a puff at his pipe and remarked, 'The lady has an obvious grasp of international economics.' He went on to say that as President he had found similar untapped resources in the Bolivian population--on one occasion a female delegation from a rural village had come sternly into his office, addressed him familiarly as 'thee' and 'thou' and 'comrade', and demanded a bridge for the village which would have cost several thousand dollars.

Despite United States aid he had not got the dollars, but he was delighted. He had reason to be. Before the revolution in which he played a leading part, Indian women used to make way on the pavement for White or *mestizo* men; now, properly enough, they expect men of any race to make way for them, and the men do. The women in bowler hats are never going to get out of anybody's way again.

# Intervention in Guatemala

IF THE UNITED STATES saw the warning light in Bolivia in 1952, it signally failed to do so in Guatemala in 1954, where Washington's intervention roused bitter memories of the days of Teddy Roosevelt and the Big Stick. Indeed it would probably be true to say that United States behaviour in Guatemala was one of the most important external factors in causing the widespread sympathy which exists today for Castro among numerous groups of Latin Americans who otherwise have no use for communism.

Like United States assistance in 1961 to the abortive invasion of Cuba at the Bay of Pigs, intervention in Guatemala was justified—indeed boasted of—as a necessary step to avoid the communization of the continent. Though many responsible North Americans have since had second thoughts it would be hard to find a single United States newspaper which did not at the time hail their government's part in the overthrow of the Arbenz government in Guatemala as a blow struck for democracy. Even today, most standard United States' works on the subject, including those produced by reputable universities, still treat this anachronistic resuscitation of the Big Stick principle as a legitimate and necessary action.

But the circumstances obtaining in Guatemala differed in many important respects from those existing in Cuba after the Castro revolution. Most importantly, the Guatemalan government, unlike many Latin American administrations of the period, had been elected constitutionally by popular vote. Guatemala was in most respects a free country, a comparatively novel experience for its citizens who had only enjoyed this luxury since 1944.

Heritage of Tyranny

Prior to this the country's three million people, *ladino* (White or *mestizo*) and *indio* had been accustomed to little but ruthless dictatorship. From 1898 to 1920 this was exercised by the *mestizo* Manuel Estrada Cabrera, a lawyer by profession who should have known better. When he was eventually deposed by an armed revolt there was no body of citizens with the experience or ability to take over power, and a period of chaos and civil strife supervened. This was followed by the dictatorship of an army officer, Jorge Ubico, of whom the best his apologists can say is that he was not quite as bad as Estrada. Nevertheless his memory is still detested today, and many people, regardless of the current régime, still refer to police headquarters as *El Castillo Maldito* or The Accursed Castle.

Ubico's fall was one of the direct effects on Latin America of World War II. Like all Latin American dictators, he sided with the Allies, not from any admiration for democracy, but because of the financial and other benefits accruing to him, if not to his country, from association with the United States. One of the favours he granted to the United States was to afford facilities for the defence of the Panama Canal (whose proximity was one of the reasons given for the 1954 intervention).

This entailed the presence in Guatemala not only of thousands of refreshingly uninhibited and free-spoken United States troops and airmen, but also of the North American propaganda apparatus, which at this period was naturally promoting the cause of democracy, the Atlantic Charter and President Roosevelt's Four Freedoms. As the United States sociologist Richard N. Adams dryly remarks:[1] 'In the Guatemala of Ubico, one did not generally advertise any freedoms, much less four of them, without evoking invidious comparisons.'

These were duly evoked, particularly among the younger Guatemaltecos, and in 1944 the elderly Ubico was wise enough to see the writing on the wall and withdrew to New Orleans. His departure was followed by the inevitable turbulence, but the Guatemaltecos had become more sophisticated since 1920, and this time the disorders crystallized into a social and political revolution whose aims were (among others) to remove the disabilities of the *indio* majority, to ensure consti-

[1] *Social Changes in Latin America Today*, Council on Foreign Relations, New York, 1960.

tutional government, and to free the country from the strangle-hold of big landowners, among whom the biggest was the United Fruit Company of Boston, Massachusetts.

**Left-of-centre Government**

In 1945 elections were held resulting in victory as President of Dr Juan José Arévalo, a left-of-centre Liberal. He has been subsequently criticized for his friendship with the Communists and the Peronistas and his hostility to the United States, but this is to judge him by Cold War standards which had nothing to do with the Guatemala which had just emerged from the nightmare of half a century of dictatorship and in which 2 per cent of the population owned 70 per cent of the land—a fact which even that doughty anti-communist Liberal, Don Salvador de Madariaga of Spain, has admitted in a recent book.[1]

In 1950 elections were held again, and won by Colonel Jacobo Arbenz Guzmán, a former army officer who had opposed Ubico, and who enjoyed the support of his predecessor Arévalo. He was not—though he now may be—a communist. But he had communist support at the polls, and believed that he could control his embarrassing allies. That this was a cause for some concern cannot be denied.

When I visited Guatemala in 1953 the Communist Party there was possibly the most powerful in Latin America—though not more powerful than the Communist Parties in France or Italy at the time. Its members held important posts in the three main political parties, though since such people naturally held no cards this is impossible to prove. On the evidence of civil servants I spoke to, they certainly had posts in some vital ministries, notably that of education. They also at the time controlled the principal trades unions, which were affiliated to the CTAL (*Confederación de Trabajadores Latino-americanos*), led by the Mexican Vicente Lombardo Toledano, which in turn was a member of the communist WFTU (World Federation of Trades Unions) rather than the rival ICFTU (International Confederation of Free Trades Unions). Practically the only important union at the time was that of the railwaymen.

[1] *Latin America Between the Eagle and the Bear*, Hollis & Carter, London, 1962.

# Intervention in Guatemala

All this may have sounded remarkably menacing to Washington. But it did not appear so to most people in Guatemala. The communist newspaper *Octubre* was sold in the streets by boys crying out, 'The Voice of the Communist Party!' The official title of *Octubre* was 'Central Organ of the Communist Party *of Guatemala*', but the news-boys left out the last bit—no doubt to save their breath, but it was a remarkably accurate omission: the leadership of the Communist Party of Guatemala was mostly composed of foreigners.

This was no doubt one of the things which most frightened Washington. The State Department at the time told me that the Communist Party of Guatemala served two functions, both international: firstly, to provide a Cominform headquarters for the Americas, since other American countries had banned or restricted communist activities; secondly, to put every possible spoke in the wheel of the United States. *Washington is worried*

At the same time they pointed out that the communists were working hard to exacerbate the dispute with Britain over the ownership of British Honduras, in order to drive a wedge between Britain and the Western Hemisphere, as the United States could not logically support publicly Britain's position in British Honduras. Finally, they added, Guatemala was the largest of the Central American nations and was their traditional leader, and whoever effectively controlled Central America also controlled the Panama Canal.

Except for the last contention, all this was more or less true —but was it important? The Guatemaltecos themselves were quite alive to the communist threat, and would not have put up with Arbenz Guzmán dragging them into any bloc, east or west. Lombardo Toledano's CTAL has long ceased to be a potent force. School-teachers can think for themselves. A railway strike would not paralyse Guatemala as it would a larger and more developed country. International communism has had its Latin American headquarters elsewhere, notably in Uruguay, without doing harm to either the country concerned or the United States.

A people newly accustomed to democracy are unlikely to

feel particularly keen to exchange one form of authoritarianism for another, as was made quite plain to me by two Guatemalan CID officers to whom I spoke. They had been engaged on the investigation of the 'thrill' murder of a taxi-driver by four gilded youths one New Year's Eve, and had been hampered in this and other legitimate jobs by what they called 'political interference'—i.e. deflection from their duties when political reasons sent them elsewhere. They were willing to forfeit their pension rights if this went on, as were other civil servants in similar circumstances. And they had their remedy at the polls. They were determined to stand up for the democracy they had won in 1944 and convinced of their power to do it for themselves.

Counter-
revolution

Nevertheless, the United States government of the time was so terrified of communism, and possibly so affected by the pressure of the United Fruit Company in its fear of nationalization, that it chose to back a reactionary invasion, launched from a neighbouring dictatorial country, and led by a ferret-faced, undistinguished and disappointed army officer, Colonel Castillo Armas.

It was a farcical decision. The Guatemalan Government, far from being a possible threat to the Panama Canal, was in no position to combat an invasion by Castillo Armas' raggle taggle army so long as the latter had United States support— Arbenz had no bombers and even his fighters were ten years old, thanks to the United States embargo on arms to his country. All he had was the general support of the people, most of them peasants, and while it may be easy to turn swords into ploughshares it is hardly feasible to turn ploughshares into machine-guns—even if you know what's happening.

The Guatemaltecos did *not* know what was happening, and nor did the CIA or the State Department. They did not realize that they were not only putting the clock back but identifying themselves with all that was hated in the emergent democracy of Latin America. To avoid any charge of hindsight in this matter I quote an article of mine published in *The Observer* on 27 June 1954 when the 'Guatemalan Affair' was still going on:

'Dr Juan Manuel Gálvez, President of Honduras, from which country the rebels admittedly launched their attack, was the single candidate at the last election in 1948. He has also for many years been the local legal representative of the United States-owned United Fruit Company, a fact to which the Guatemalans, perhaps unkindly, attach some importance.

'Nevertheless, tiny Guatemala . . . has some reason for being apprehensive of the powerful influence of United Fruit, which is the largest business not only in Guatemala but in almost all the other Central American countries, as well as having large interests in Colombia or elsewhere. It owns or leases 2,500,000 acres in the Caribbean area and employs over 90,000 people. Its net earnings in 1953 were $44,500,000, and in Guatemala it virtually controls the railway system—an important matter in a country with utterly inadequate highways. In the circumstances the Guatemalan belief that the State Department may be unduly influenced by the views of United Fruit is understandable.

'On their side, the North Americans are, equally understandably, frightened by the power of the Guatemalan Communist Party . . . the extent of communist influence is disquieting though not so disquieting in a Latin American setting as it might be elsewhere. Latin America, on the face of it, presents an ideal field for communist activity. There is almost everywhere a wide gap between rich and poor. . . . Many Latin Americans are living at subsistence level, millions are illiterate and easily indoctrinated, and among the intelligentsia, for cultural and historical reasons, anti-*yanqui* sentiment is strong.

'Nevertheless, communism has never yet really taken hold of a Latin American nation. In Argentina before Perón the political leadership of the Left was taken by the Socialists, and trades unionism was largely anarchist or syndicalist. In Uruguay the communists had a brief heyday in the twenties, which achieved little more than the disestablishment of the Roman Catholic Church. In Brazil after World War II the party succeeded in infiltrating the higher ranks of the army, but President Getulio Vargas averted the danger by judicious postings, promotions and demotions. In Chile in 1946 the communists, who are powerful in the unions, obtained two Cabinet posts in return for electoral support for Dr González Videla, but lost them when they proved obstructive, and are now outlawed by the Defence of Democracy Act.

'In Mexico Moscow was forestalled by the agrarian revolution of 1910, and, despite the later activities of the trade union leader Lombardo Toledano, sympathy was forfeited by clumsy Russian tactics. In Peru leftist sentiment rallied round APRA . . . led by Victor Raúl Haya de la Torre. He is now in exile in Mexico, and his party is proscribed, but the local, ineffectually-led Communist Party has been unable to fill the vacuum.

'This widespread lack of success is due partly to the enormous influence of the Roman Catholic Church, partly to the naturally conservative nature of the peasant farmers who still make up the majority of Latin America's population. It is even affected by a natural interest in the supposed material benefits of the "American way of life".

'But most of all, perhaps, Latin Americans are swayed by nationalism which sometimes verges on the parochial. National Sovereignty with capital initials, means to Latin Americans rather what the Crown means to Britons. The sentiment with which they invest their sense of statehood inclines them to the view that communists, being somehow foreign, are not of great importance. It is on this belief that the non-communist members of the Guatemalan government base their rather light-hearted attitude to the Party; Guatemalans, they believe, are first and foremost Guatemalans.

'It is this intense feeling for sovereignty which has been most deeply aroused by the United States attitude towards the Guatemalan question. Latin Americans do not see this as an attack on communism, but as an interference with the domestic affairs of an independent sovereign state by a country too large to be successfully opposed. The speeches of Mr Dulles and Mr Cabot Lodge bring back memories of United States intervention in Mexico, Haiti, Nicaragua and the Dominican Republic, and harm North America's reputation south of the River Bravo.

'If the Arbenz régime in Guatemala is overthrown no Latin American country will feel the same towards the United States as before: the United States will be more feared, less loved. If it succeeds in defeating the rebels, United States prestige will have suffered a severe blow. It looks as though the United States would have done better to leave this matter alone. Until now, the Latinos have always shown themselves capable of shrugging off their communists, of muddling through, provided they are left alone to do so.'

Subsequent events proved this all too true. Even the countries and governments in Latin America most friendly towards the United States found themselves unable to qualify or condone an intervention which had put into power a régime reminiscent of those which had plagued the continent for over a century. The Guatemalans themselves felt much the same, and not without reason.

*Alienating Latin America*

Castillo Armas sought public approval and international endorsement by holding an election in which it was only possible to vote 'Yes' or 'No'—thus acting rather more like the communists than his allegedly communist predecessors. He got his 'Yes'—not surprisingly, since the ballot was far from secret. In 1957 he was assassinated by a member of the palace guard, who had joined this *élite* corps for precisely that purpose, thinking it important enough to sacrifice his own life for it.

Castillo Armas has been succeeded in the presidency by Miguel Ydígoras Fuentes, a temperamental person who has tangled frequently with Britain and Mexico and blames most of his troubles on Castro. But he has not been entirely a fool, though some of his opponents charitably consider him insane: he has refrained from putting back the clock to the extent of depriving the peasants of the lands which they gained as a result of the 1944 revolution, and he has not returned the control of local communities to the power of the former landlords.

Inside Guatemala therefore, it is improbable that conditions will ever return to the dark days of Estrada and Ubico. To this extent, the panicky action of the United States in 1954 has done less harm than might be expected. But outside Guatemala, in the rest of the American continent, it probably did more to alienate thinking Latin Americans from the United States and to further the cause of communism in the Western Hemisphere than any single action the United States has ever taken. For the communists, in Guatemala, were on the side of the very kind of development which President Kennedy deems necessary for a country to qualify for the *Alianza para Progreso* —and which is in fact necessary if Latin America is to take her place in the twentieth-century world.

# The Middle-Class Revolt

THE GUATEMALAN REVOLT OF 1944 differed in only one respect from the political changes, violent or peaceful, which many Latin American countries went through at the period of Allied victory in World War II—it anticipated the victory itself by a year. Otherwise it represented the same surge of anger against dictatorship which occurred elsewhere, and was supported in the same way by all of the population which did not have a vested interest in the former régime.

All these revolutions were basically leftist, and their success was due to the support of the working classes, even where, as with the election of Perón in Argentina, the eventual result was a dictatorship where none had been before. The years 1944–46 in most of Latin America saw the proletariat on the march, sometimes quite literally, as did the Bolivian Revolution of 1952 and the Cuban Revolution of 1959.

Most subsequent revolutions, however, though they differed in many respects from each other, were sharply differentiated from the movements of the mid-forties in that they were basically middle-class. The forces which overthrew Perón in Argentina in 1955, Rojas Pinilla in Colombia in 1957, and Pérez Jiménez in Venezuela in 1958, had support from many sections of the population, but the motive power came from the bourgeoisie. Apart from the fact that the Communists, who in Latin America are mostly of bourgeois origin themselves, use the word 'bourgeoisie' as a pejorative term, there is a widespread belief abroad that this stratum of the population does not exist in Latin America, or that it is so small that it doesn't matter. This belief is even shared by many Latin Americans who have visible evidence to the contrary and who may, like the Communist leaders, belong themselves to his allegedly non-existent class.

Who are these middle-class Latin Americans? And how have they come to carry out at least three bourgeois revolutions

*Bourgeois revolutions*

*later* than several proletarian ones, thus confounding Karl Marx and apparently reversing in a local context the sequence of events in Europe between 1789 and 1917?

The middle class as such is not a new phenomenon in Latin America. It grew up of necessity along with the Iberian colonies. In all of these there had to be storekeepers, overseers, traders, apothecaries, clerks and middlemen of all kinds—jobs which were beneath the dignity of the Spaniards and Portuguese, even if they could have done them, and beyond the range of *indios* or Negro slaves, who would not have been permitted to do them if they could.

Mixed ethnic groups    In largely Indian nations like Peru and Ecuador the gap came to be filled by the *mestizos*—which suited everybody all round since the *mestizos* considered themselves too superior to associate with the humble *indios*, yet were on the whole not accepted socially by the Europeans. This situation to a great extent exists to this day, with the addition of *mulatos* and other mixed ethnic groups to the *mestizo* ranks, though many present-day *mestizos* consider themselves and are considered white, and I know at least two *mulato* middle-class families in Peru who consider themselves, perhaps on the North American analogy, to be Negroes.

These people are quite aware of the part they play in the community. I was in Lima at a time when the South African government enacted legislation banning Coloureds, or people of mixed racial origin, from a number of skilled occupations. A Peruvian *mestizo* remarked to me:

'If they did that here we should have chaos. The lights would all go out and the trams would stop running for lack of electricians. The hospitals would close for lack of nurses. We should have hardly any engine-drivers, shop assistants, waiters or mechanics. The airlines would have no ground-crews and the armed forces hardly any NCOs. We would be left with a handful of landowners and lawyers and millions of illiterate peasants. We'd be back in the eighteenth century.'

In areas like Argentina, Chile, Uruguay and Southern Brazil, where the *indio* population was sparse and Negro slavery played only a small part in the economy, the place of the *mestizo* in the social hierarchy tended to be occupied by European immigrants from countries other than Spain and Portugal. These, particularly the British, were on the whole uninterested in local social distinctions, and indeed often considered themselves superior to 'dagoes' of whatever pretensions, but they were extremely interested in making money.

The Brazilian sociologist Gilberto Preyre, quoting a contemporary British visitor, writes in his book *Ingleses no Brasil* that

The British
Community

> '. . . the English residents in Brazil in 1821 were already numerous. . . . In Rio de Janeiro the British colony included "respectable merchants, besides tradesmen, artisans and others". Owners of shops in rua Dereita, rua da Alfândega, rua dos Pescados, as well as blacksmiths, shoemakers, tailors, jewellers.'

Although there were some 'adventurers' among the British community, there were many who settled with their families and whose descendants are solid citizens of modern Brazil.

This early settlement of middle-class Britons was even more notable in Argentina, and indeed had some official encouragement from the British end. In 1826 the British envoy to the Río de la Plata, Lord Ponsonby, wrote to the Foreign Secretary, George Canning,

> 'The Settler finds here an abundance of Horse and Cattle, a rich soil, and a constant and easy communication with England: Religion [i.e. Protestantism] not only tolerated but respected; and persons and property as well protected as the persons and property of the native inhabitants, and a prospect, almost a certainty, that by industry and skill a considerable fortune may be rapidly accumulated.'

Ponsonby foresaw a rapid growth of the British community, and he was right. Following the original merchants came the personnel of the British-owned railways, banks, insurance companies, waterworks, gas companies and tramways. Many of these remained in the country and raised families, thus increasing the prosperous middle class. Some families, it is true, remained for generations, and still remain, outside the main stream of Argentine national life, but others intermarried or became *acriollados*. All had an effect on the country's developing social structure, and the institutions they served (some now nationalized) absorbed a growing number of Argentines whose forebears would have regarded such occupations as degrading.

The Irish, the Scots and the Welsh also arrived in considerable numbers and made their contribution to the growing bourgeoisie, as did the Dutch in Tres Arroyos and the Germans around Córdoba and elsewhere. The Germans also settled in the Brazilian States of Río Grande do Sul and Santa Catalina, and in Southern Chile around Valdivia and Concepción, while in the present century cities like São Paulo and Buenos Aires have attracted largely middle-class immigration from all over Europe.

Italian immigration

But it was the huge Italian immigration in the latter part of the last century which basically altered the social pattern of the southern part of the continent. Most Italian immigrants were poor and often illiterate on arrival, but in the New World they eagerly grasped the opportunities denied to them at home, and in many cases rose from rags to comparative riches in a single generation. Initially even the most successful were looked down upon by the *criollo* 'aristocracy', but more and more ordinary citizens were moved by their example to break out of the class into which they had been born, an ascent which became easier with the spread of State education.

All this of course applies principally to the larger and more temperate countries. The process was much less marked in Northern South America, in the Caribbean and in Central America, and in Mexico it only started, paradoxically, with the 'institutionalization' of what had initially been a peasants' and workers' revolution (the same paradox is probably true of the Soviet Union). But, as a result of such factors as the discovery of oil in Venezuela, the emergence of local industries in places like Medellín in Colombia, the enlargement of universities, improved and cheaper communications, and the lure of consumer goods advertised on radio and television, more and more Latin Americans are moving into the middle class.

At first sight these would hardly seem to constitute the stuff of which revolutions are made. In the large urban areas many commute daily by train, tram or bus, and increasingly by car—often locally made or assembled. They live in suburban houses with small gardens, or blocks of flats in city centres, or somewhere between the two, in terraced rows of Spanish-Victorian dwellings with tall rooms built around *patios*. More of them employ maids than would be the case in Europe, and they grumble about the servant problem (the more advanced the country, the more acute the problem). The men carry briefcases and their wives play canasta; they read more books than their English equivalents and tend to disdain television sets or to be apologetic about them ('The children like to watch "The Lone Ranger" '). Many of them follow the fortunes of a local football team; they belong to country clubs or yacht clubs of varying degrees of exclusiveness; their teen-age children make liberal use of the telephone. They are not, in the usual sense of the word, at all revolutionary.

But, in another sense, they are. By and large, they are the first or second generation to lead this kind of life—they have only just reached the position reached by the European and North American middle classes one or two generations ago. To them, their status is a sign of the progress of their particular country, and they are liable to look on the advance of the working classes as a threat to their position rather than to accept it with good grace or otherwise as an inevitability. At the same time they are frightened of the frequent demagoguery of the leftist leaders, which leads them to believe they are in danger of escaping from the old *caudillismo* of the right only to find themselves under a dictatorship of the left.

Status

This was particularly evident during the administration of Perón in Argentina, when the middle class, basically concerned with preserving its own relatively privileged position against the proletariat, found itself allied with other groups with different reasons for disliking Perón: the liberals of all parties who deplored dictatorship; the Socialists who resented their loss of control of the labour movement; the Army whose attitude has been mentioned earlier; and the Catholics who were outraged by Perón's interference with the Church.

In Colombia the situation two years later was similar, with one important exception; though Rojas Pinilla was largely removed by middle-class efforts, organized labour and the working class generally were as opposed to the dictatorship as anyone else, so that the revolution was in fact a national revolution. This was true too of Venezuela in 1958, though the leadership of the revolution was in this case in the hands of the Socialist *Acción Democrática*. Nevertheless the present Venezuelan Government is beset with the same opposition from the left which has faced all Argentine Governments since the fall of Perón.

In effect all these middle-class revolutions are likely to be merely interim solutions, and are in due course bound to give way to more radical forces. This is underlined by the fact that the organized students, themselves largely middle class and always a factor in Latin American politics, are on the whole well to the left of their parents and their Governments. This is true particularly of Venezuela, but the same phenomenon can be observed in countries which have had no political upheavals, such as Chile and Uruguay. Throughout Latin America a majority of students has at least an emotional sympathy with Fidel Castro in Cuba, as well as often an intellectual leaning towards Marxism; the implications of this will be discussed in the next two chapters.

# Part Three

## THE CUBAN REVOLUTION

# The Rise of Castro

It is difficult to remember today that when Fidel Castro's victorious *barbudos* marched into Havana on New Year's Day 1959, the event was acclaimed with few reservations in almost every country in the world. In part this was due to the repulsive nature of the régime they had overthrown, in part to the character of Castro himself, as far as it could be judged.

On 2 January 1959 the Manchester *Guardian* said editorially: 'What Dr Castro will make of his opportunities is far from clear; some of his proclamations have been radical in tone, but that is not uncommon with the "Outs" in Latin America.' On 3 January the London *Times* said: 'Dr Castro has proved himself to be an inspired military leader, and it is to be hoped that his courage and other qualities will help him to face perhaps more subtle enemies in the political field. . . . Yet the best guarantee for peace and quiet in Cuba in the probably very uncertain future is Dr Castro himself; that is what he has fought for fanatically in the last two and a half years.'

The editorial ended: 'A longer term problem for Cuba is economic. By disrupting communications and even burning the sugar plantations the rebel movement has succeeded in virtually bringing Cuba's economy to a standstill. This tragic situation is a challenge to pan-Americanism and one which might well be taken up by the Organization of American States.'—An ironical suggestion to read now, when Castro has denounced the Organization of American States to which all the American Republics belong, as a tool of *yanqui* imperialism. Yet at that time the United States Press was as enthusiastic about Castro's success as the *Guardian* and the *Times*.

Before discussing why the North Americans soon changed their minds, it is necessary to study the reasons for their reaction, and that of the rest of the non-communist world, in 1959.

Cuba had had a very different history from the other Latin American countries, having achieved its independence from Spain only in 1901. An earlier attempt to win it had been made under the patriot José Martí, Cuba's national hero, but it had been a gallant failure. When independence finally did come, though the Cubans had fought as bravely as before, it was largely as a result of the Spanish-American War which broke out in 1898 and in which the United States was victorious. This was during the period of the 'Big Stick', when the United States was going through the imperialist phase associated with the words 'Manifest Destiny', and as a result of the war she annexed the former Spanish colonies of Puerto Rico and the Philippine Islands.

Illusory independence

Cuba escaped this fate, but her independence proved in fact to be little more than a disguised form of colonialism, exemplified in the Platt Amendment to the Cuban Constitution, by which the United States had final fiscal authority in Cuba and had the right to intervene militarily in the country at any time this seemed in the interests of the Cuban people *as interpreted by the President of the United States*. This amendment was accepted by a puppet constituent assembly in Havana at a time when the city was still garrisoned by United States forces. The strategic reason for these restrictions on Cuban sovereignty was presumably the desire to protect the isthmus of Panama where the United States was shortly to start building an interoceanic canal. This intention was underlined by a further provision of the amendment permitting the United States to build and occupy a naval base at Guantánamo, for which rent would be paid but which would in every other sense be under United States sovereignty.

However much sense all this may have made to United States naval and military planners at the time (and a good deal more recently), in the long run it went far to cause the Cuban resentment which in part fed the fires of the *Fidelista* revolution and eventually made Cuba the first Latin American country to break all its ties with the United States and to team up with the Soviet bloc.

The rest of the Constitution was naturally based, like that of many freer Latin Republics, on the Constitution of the United States. There was the separation of powers between the Executive, the Legislature and the Judiciary. The President was to be elected by direct suffrage, and there were two Houses of Congress. Education was to be free and compulsory, and Church and State were separated. There was in fact the whole façade of North American democracy, but it was only a façade.

Even in North America itself, individual States have constantly gone against the spirit of the document subscribed to by the Founding Fathers, but there has always been the force of national public opinion and the power of the Federal Government to ensure some kind of compliance. In Cuba neither of these checks existed: public opinion was resentful, ill-informed, and virtually powerless; the nearest approach to Federal authority was that of the United States itself, and Washington was a good deal less interested in the rights and freedoms of the Cuban people than in the favourable treatment of United States interests on the island, who hastened to make friends with the powerful Spanish-descended landowners whose position was scarcely altered by the change of sovereignty.

(It is only fair to say the great majority of the United States public, ill-served in this respect by most of the Press, was totally unaware of this situation and believed their country to have truly liberated Cuba. This ignorance was one of the factors responsible for the nation-wide indignation at Fidel Castro's actions when he achieved power.)

In the circumstances in which Cuba was placed, it was not surprising that few patriotic Cubans felt inclined to go into national politics, and those Cubans who did choose a political career were motivated rather more by personal ambition and the hope of gain than are most politicians. Those who had higher motives soon resigned or were shouldered aside. The history of Cuba from 'independence' until Castro's victory is thus one of cynicism, corruption, coercion and constant political change, during which the rich grew richer and the poor remained as they were.

Cynicism
and
corruption

During this period Cuba was twice occupied by United States Marines, and between 1906 and 1908 came under direct United States rule as a result of a request for 'advice' from the Cuban Government. These interventions, far from having a stabilizing effect on the country, tended to exacerbate the political insecurity. In 1925, with the accession of Gerado Machado, a so-called Liberal, to the Presidency, all pretence at democracy came to an end. In 1927 Machado hand-picked a new constitutional convention which repealed the clause preventing a President from succeeding himself and extended the Presidential term from four to six years. In 1928 elections were held at which, foreseeably, Machado was returned for a second term.

Once securely in power he followed the example of the less savoury *caudillos* on the mainland. When the Wall Street slump hit Cuba in 1929, Machado cut the salaries of civil servants, but at the same time increased the size of the armed forces (whose job in the circumstances could only be repressive) and gave well-paid jobs to his friends. When members of the Radical Opposition protested in 1930, they were charged with sedition and deported. When, shortly after, students of Havana University paraded in protest, the parade was brutally broken up by the police, touching off student riots. Machado's tame Congress thereupon suspended all constitutional guarantees, and the Government closed the University, arresting and imprisoning both undergraduates and members of the Faculty.

'Haves' and 'Have-nots'

At this point the Supreme Court, taking seriously the independence of the Judiciary, belatedly declared unconstitutional all laws passed since 1928. Machado ignored the ruling, and an abortive revolution broke out in 1931. Finally Machado was ousted in 1933 less by the strength of his opponents than by a change of heart in Washington, where Franklin D. Roosevelt had now become President, and for a time at least dictatorial régimes had gone out of favour. Without United States support Machado could not last, and he fled—ironically, to the United States.

The fall of Machado did not, however, mean the emergence of democracy in Cuba, for the system was unchanged. Politics was still confined largely to Havana, and in Havana to the 'haves', of whatever political colour. The seasonally-employed sugar-cane cutters living in their flimsy *bohíos*, the *peones* on the cattle ranches, the tobacco-workers, and the thousands of slum-dwellers in Havana itself, were almost as far outside the stream of national life as the Quéchua and Aymara Indians of Bolivia. The middle-class politicians started once again their private game of intrigue and corruption, accusation and counter-accusation, and not surprisingly soon landed themselves with another dictator, Fulgencio Batista.

Batista was a former Army sergeant who had headed an NCOs' revolt which had been partially responsible for the overthrow of Machado. Self-promoted to General, he became the most powerful figure in the Army, and as such had no difficulty in becoming President for a four-year term in 1940. In 1944 he stepped down, as demanded by the 1901 Constitution, but in fact he never let go the reins of power, and in 1952 he deposed the elected President, Carlos Prío Socarrás and openly took charge himself.

To an outside world preoccupied with a World War and a Cold War following on its heels, Batista was what Richard Dimbleby once called him on the BBC a 'tin-pot dictator', the pretentious little ruler of an insignificant country, of rather less serious news-value than Prince Rainier of Monaco. To thousands of United States tourists thronging the beaches and the luxury hotels of Havana his name was scarcely known—unlike some of his contemporaries he realized that personality-cults are bad for the tourist trade, on which pre-Castro Cuba relied heavily. To many North American businessmen he was the kind of a guy you could do business with, to mutual advantage. But to Cubans he was a ruthless and corrupt dictator whose henchmen tore out people's fingernails, lived on the earnings of prostitution, and made decent citizens both frightened and ashamed.

One young citizen, however, was more ashamed than most, and he was *not* frightened. In 1942, when Batista officially took control, Fidel Castro was a post-graduate law student at the

University of Havana. Though he was later to become the symbol of the emancipation of the working classes he came, like so many revolutionaries, from a thoroughly bourgeois background. Though his father had started his working life as a labourer for the United Fruit Company of Boston he rose to become the proprietor of a sugar estate and married a member of Cuba's rural aristocracy. By the time Fidel was born in 1927 the family was prosperous and respected among the 'right' people in the neighbourhood of Santiago de Cuba, in the eastern part of the island.

**Fidel Castro's early days**

These circles, however, were far removed from the bickering politicians of the capital, whom they thoroughly despised. At the same time, as sugar producers, they were resentful of their dependence on the United States market, and as Cubans of their political subservience to the United States. Finally, Fidel grew up during the dictatorship of the detested Machado. All these factors, plus a youthful idealism, served to mould a plantation-owner's son into a revolutionary—without the idealism he might well have become a delinquent (some of his critics, of course, would say that he did).

He was educated at Jesuit colleges in Santiago de Cuba and Havana, the equivalent of British prep school and public school education with some overtones of a 'colonial' missionary upbringing. Unlike many revolutionaries with a religious schooling, including Juárez in Mexico, he did not react by becoming a violent anti-clerical: rather he came to regard the Church as irrelevant, except where it seemed to him to be mixing in politics.

Politics became his passion as soon as he entered the University. This was true of perhaps the majority of his fellow undergraduates, but Fidel was prepared to do more than talk, and he was soon arrested for joining a group who intended to mount an expedition against Rafael Trujillo, the dictator of the Dominican Republic. He was released and went on studying for his MA and then his doctorate, but his rage against the Cuban *status quo* never abated.

On 26 July 1953, the tall, brown-eyed ascetic-looking and

still beardless young man led an angry, crazy revolt against the Batista barracks in Santiago de Cuba. It failed, as it was bound to do. So complete was the failure that Batista, after clerical intercession, decided to treat the whole thing as a childish joke, and refrained from torturing or executing Castro; he merely imprisoned him. But, despite Batista's contempt and his own failure, the date of Castro's abortive revolution became a symbol to Cubans of opposition to dictatorship and corruption.

In 1955, Castro was released under a general amnesty and went into exile, first in the United States and then—more to his taste—in Mexico. In both places he met plotters against the régime, comfortable exiles living in places like Miami, forming shadow governments, and having *emigré* squabbles among themselves. He realized that these were not the people to fire the inspiration of a nation and build a new Cuba. The only way to do that was to fight, and the only place to fight was in Cuba.

On 26 December 1956, he landed from a yacht on the coast of Oriente, his own province, with some eighty like-minded young men, calling themselves the Twenty-sixth of July Movement, in memory of the attack on Santiago barracks. The weather was against them, their arrival was delayed for two days, and they landed in a swamp. The word had been passed to Batista, and his trained, professional troops moved in and wiped out all but twelve of the would-be revolutionaries. But the remainder, amazingly, were not disheartened.

They took to the mountains and gradually gathered a core of guerrilla fighters around them, of all classes and both sexes. They trained them on the lines of the Yugoslav partisans and the French *maquis*. They disappeared by day and attacked by night. They ran rings around Batista's heavily armoured troops, who had weapons supplied by the United States (for 'Hemisphere Defence') and the promise of more from Britain (as part of the export drive). They built up their force from twelve to five hundred to one thousand, and to an eventual estimated three thousand, with countless quiet local supporters and a few fifth columnists in key positions in Havana and elsewhere.

The
Revolution
begins

# The Revolutions of Latin America

To embarrass Batista they burned sugar estates (starting symbolically with Castro's own), blew up power stations, cut railway lines, and carried out hazardous stunts like the polite kidnapping of Juan Fangio, the motor-racing world champion from Argentina. They made rendezvous with sympathetic journalists like Herbert Matthews of the *New York Times*, thus publicizing their cause to the world and preparing the warm climate of opinion which greeted their ultimate success.

Even in the short term this publicity paid off. Sympathizers all over Latin America smuggled them arms and whipped up support. In Venezuela, after Pérez Jiménez was overthrown in January 1958, the *Sección Venezuela del Movimiento 26 de Julio* took space in the newspapers to advertise for Cuban and Venezuelan volunteers, and got them.

This was a far cry from the palace *coups* and military *putsches* of former days; it was a national movement with international backing. Yet at no time prior to Castro's military victory did any of this backing, at home or abroad, come from the Communist Party. Some of the members of the movement, notably Castro's principal lieutenant, the Argentine Dr Ernesto 'Ché' Guevara, and his fanatical younger brother, Raúl Castro, made no secret of their Marxism, and in Raúl's case of his detestation of everything 'Made in the United States of America', and Fidel himself was as liable to quote Lenin as José Martí. But official Communism remained aloof.

**The Cuban Communists**

The Cuban Communist Party, though it now likes to forget it, was if anything on the other side, and had been for a long time. Throughout the 'thirties, 'forties and most of the 'fifties the Communist Parties of Latin America tended to support the forces of repression, however rightist they might be, partly for 'tactical' reasons and partly from a doctrinaire refusal to have any truck with 'bourgeois' or 'social democratic' movements. It may also be that with their monolithic structure, particularly during the Stalin period, they found it easier to deal with dictators than with argumentative democrats.

In any case, the Cuban Party was no exception. Though its chairman, Blas Roca, is of Cuban working-class background,

126

he has never found any difficulty in following the shifts of Moscow policy, however personally distasteful some of them must have been to him. In 1933, as an official of the Communist-dominated shoe-workers' union, he tried to make a deal with Machado to increase the Party's then almost negligible influence. At that time almost the whole of the country's labour force was on strike against the dictatorship, and Machado's terms were that if the Communists denounced the strike they would be given control of the CTC (Cuban Confederation of Labour). Blas Roca accepted. Four days later the dictatorship was overthrown.

A Party purge followed, but Roca himself survived it, no doubt because Moscow wanted at least one genuine worker in the party leadership. At any rate, he was invited to the Soviet Union as a delegate to the Seventh Congress of the Comintern, and on his return was made Secretary-General of the Cuban Party, a post he has held ever since. He immediately took up where he had left off, and started negotiations with Batista.

As a first concession for Communist support, Batista allowed the Party to start publishing its newspaper *Hoy* (Today), and, when this refrained from criticizing him, gave the Communists what they really wanted, control of the CTC—though how useful this really was in the circumstances it is difficult to say. In any case, when Batista ended his first Presidential term in 1944 and allowed his elected successor, Ramón Grau San Martín, to take office, he did nothing to prevent him from ousting the Party from control of the labour movement and hamstringing it in other ways, a policy continued by his successor Prío Socarrás. When Batista openly took power again in 1952 the Cold War had already replaced the war-time alliance against the Axis, and to avoid offending the United States, whose tourism and sugar imports formed the basis of Cuban economy, Batista outlawed the Communist Party.

During all this period, whatever its technical position, the Party had never enjoyed any significant measure of popular support. Despite the impeccably Cuban background of its Secretary-General, despite efforts to give it a 'Cuban face' by a

An alien
organization

127

change of vocabulary and a soft-pedalling of criticisms of the Catholic Church, the Party remained to most Cubans an alien organization—and its flirtations with two dictatorships were not forgotten. From 1956 onwards, after the guerrilla war had begun, any hopes of reform which might have been placed on the Communists were transferred to the Twenty-sixth of July Movement, which appealed not only to the dispossessed and the leftist intelligentsia but also to thousands of disgruntled and disgusted members of the middle classes.

In a way there was a parallel with what had happened in China, where the Russian Communists had urged their Chinese colleagues to follow the classic Marxist policy of organizing the urban workers, getting control of the cities, and consolidating the countryside afterwards. The Chinese took no notice, based their revolution on the rural areas, and proved to be triumphantly right. So did Castro.

In 1959, for the first time in Cuba, a revolution occurred in which Havana had no hand at all. When the flower-bedecked tanks rolled into Havana and girls flung their arms round the grimy, bearded, battledressed troops, it marked the end of an epoch in Cuban history. Fidel, and a nation in arms, had triumphed, while the traditional leadership of the left had stood on the sidelines. The only real aid Havana had given had been the defection of Batistiano troops who were not prepared to fight their fellow-countrymen.

The numerically insignificant Communist Party might have been expected to be not only discredited but done for. But the Communists are resilient, and, though they seldom admit it, they learn from their mistakes. As a result of Castro's victory in Cuba they changed their entire strategy in Latin America, and in doing so successfully they were greatly helped by the mistakes of others, notably the Government of the United States.

# From Victory to Invasion

NOW THAT CUBA HAS BECOME a source of bitter contention in Latin America, and of embarrassment and anxiety to both sides in the Cold War, it is a little startling to realize how slowly this pattern developed.

On 6 January 1959, the day before Fidel himself reached Havana, Dr Manuel Urrutia, a respectable lawyer who as a judge had courageously opposed Batista, was appointed President-Designate, a move which encouraged all those who hoped for a democratic outcome to the Cuban revolution. Britain, among others, promptly recognized the new régime.

On 12 January the shooting began. Seventy-one supporters of the Batista Government, mostly police officers, soldiers and spies, were executed by firing squads for crimes against humanity, after summary courts martial. United States Senator Wayne Morse (Democrat from Oregon) appealed to Castro's men to postpone judgement until passions had cooled. The new Cuban authorities replied in effect that such summary justice was necessary if those who had suffered under Batista were not to take the law into their own hands and possibly lynch innocent people. The executions continued over the following months, sometimes involving the innocent people they were supposed to protect, and did more to antagonize ordinary North Americans than the Cubans themselves ever realized. Much of the blame, rightly or wrongly, was laid at the door of Fidel's brother Raúl, who was swiftly identified by the United States Press as a Communist.

Nevertheless, on 16 April Fidel himself went to Washington on a good-will visit. He was given no red carpet, literally or figuratively, but was received with a certain guarded courtesy. Even *Time* magazine, to which he subsequently became anathema, while it took care to mention his 'leftist and fellow-traveller network' (almost synonymous terms to many North Americans) had this to say, more or less in his favour:

Castro in
Washington

129

'When Castro was fighting Dictator Fulgencio Batista in Cuba's eastern mountains, he advertised his revolution's aims as a purge of governmental and social corruption and a restoration of justice and democracy. He has carried out the purge, effectively cutting off official corruption and cutting down on the once flagrant prostitution. He has curbed Cuba's feverish gambling by turning the government lottery into a savings institute and confining Havana's gaudy (but currently mostly empty) casinos to the relatively few tourists who brave the new régime's occasional, brusque clothing searches at Havana airport.'

It was, perhaps, the last tribute latent United States Puritanism was to pay to the austerity which lay behind the Cuban revolution. The following month Castro attended a conference in Buenos Aires, without causing any particular stir—probably the last time *that* could have happened in a Latin American capital.

In June, Cuba and the Dominican Republic broke off relations—the first rupture with a 'Western' country. But since the dictatorial Dominican régime of *El Benefactor* Rafael Trujillo was almost as unpopular with Washington as it was with Moscow, this particular event caused little complaint from anyone, especially as other American nations had taken the same step earlier. At the beginning of the next month the Cuban Government made a friendly approach to the United States about the sugar trade. At this period there was little evidence of orthodox Communism in Cuba, and the occasional Russian visitor was regarded almost as askance as a man from Mars.

Change for the worse

On 25 July the moderate President Urrutia was replaced by Dr Osvaldo Dorticós, widely regarded as a man of straw, and in the United States the change was regarded as ominous, presaging a total Castro dictatorship, particularly by those who had long equated Castro with Communism. By their repeated utterances to this effect these last were doing much to drive the two groups into each other's arms. Despite growing tension, however, individual United States citizens were still treated amicably in Cuba, and most Cubans when asked declared firmly that they were Fidelistas and *not* Communists.

During August, September and October there were alarms in Cuba over alleged hostile landings and acts of sabotage in which the United States was accused of complicity, in intemperate terms and often without real evidence, though Cubans now point out that subsequent events justified their fears. But if the Cuban charges were intemperate, the United States reaction was of a kind to put up the backs of any Latin American nation. Though framed in conventional diplomatic language, it was bound to appear to its proud revolutionary recipients as pompous, cliché-ridden, disingenuous, and above all patronizing.

Here are some extracts from the official report of the United States Information Service of 28 October 1959:

'Ambassador Philip W. Bonsal called on President Osvaldo Dorticós in Havana who was accompanied by Minister of State Raúl Roa to express the serious concern of the Government of the United States about the current state of relations between the United States and Cuba. Ambassador Bonsal informed the President and the Minister of State that he had been instructed to express his Government's preoccupation over what seemed to be deliberate and concerted efforts in Cuba to replace the traditional friendship between the Cuban and American people with distrust and hostility which are alien to the expressed desire of both Governments to maintain good relations. He expressed the hope that the Government of Cuba, in fulfilment of its share of the responsibility for the maintenance of good relations, would earnestly review its position in order that the traditional friendship of the two countries . . . might be restored before further damage is done. . . .

'Ambassador Bonsal made it clear that the sympathetic interest which the people and Government of the United States had taken in the freedom and well-being of the Cuban people and nation antedated the founding of the Cuban

Republic and remained the basic attitude and policy of this country towards Cuba. He pointed out the sacrifice of American lives jointly with those of Cuban patriots in the achievement of Cuban independence and the many contributions which private United States individuals and enterprises had since made to the progress of Cuba. He also expressed to the President the appreciation which the Government and the people of the United States have felt and continue to feel towards the Cuban people and nation for their loyal alliance with the United States in defence of democracy and freedom in two world wars[1] and their satisfaction with the mutually beneficial relationship of good neighbours which has existed for more than half a century. . . .

'Ambassador Bonsal . . . also underscored that the United States, in every proper way, had sought to show its understanding and sympathy with the aspirations for honest, efficient government, for the perfection of the democratic process and for economic development leading toward higher living standards and full employment. He said that these were goals which the people of Cuba share with the peoples of the United States and other free nations and which in fact distinguish these free nations from the totalitarian dictatorships which have been imposed elsewhere in the world.

'With respect to specific issues about which distortions and misunderstandings have become current in Cuba, Ambassador Bonsal informed the President and Minister of State as follows:

'(1). *The United States has observed, and will continue to observe, a policy of non-intervention in the internal affairs of Cuba and enforce, to the best of its ability, the Neutrality Act, the Customs laws and other legislation which prohibit certain activities against foreign governments by persons resident in the United States, including citizens of Cuba who have sought refuge in Florida and elsewhere in the United States. By so doing this Government is also fulfilling its obligations as a member of the OAS.*'[2]

[1] Cuba took no active part in either war. J.H.F.
[2] My italics. J.H.F.

Mr Bonsal went on to deny that a plane which had dropped leaflets on Havana the week before had come from the United States and to express 'horror and amazement' that it should have been accused of 'bombing' the capital. (There may have been an honest confusion here: the Spanish word *bombardear* can mean both literally to bomb and figuratively to bombard.) He assured President Dorticós that the United States 'deeply deplored' incidents of this kind, but that it wasn't responsible for them anyway. The Ambassador went on to point out that the United States policy of not licensing the export of arms to the Caribbean area (as from 1958) was for fear of their misuse in general, and not directed against Cuba—an assertion which must have appeared strange to Dr Dorticós in view of the use to which Batista had put United States arms prior to the 1958 embargo.

Mr Bonsal further disclaimed any responsibility for the independent Press and wire services of the United States, and denied in any case that they had engaged in a deliberate campaign to denigrate Cuba. This was, of course, perfectly true, but ignored the fact that the two major United States news agencies which spread the news of Cuba throughout the world (including most of Latin America) naturally reflected the United States viewpoint, which was at the time becoming increasingly anti-Castro. It might have been better to admit this frankly and ask what the Cubans would suggest should be done. As it was, the Cubans didn't believe a word of it, and later started their own agency, *Prensa Latina*, which has become as committed to one side in the Cold War as the Associated Press and United Press International are to the other.

The United States Ambassador went on to assure Dr Dorticós that his Government was not opposed to the economic and social reforms being undertaken by the Cuban Government. Unhappily, instead of leaving it at that, Mr Bonsal (as no doubt instructed from Washington) went on to talk about social progress within a free society, the deep sympathy with which the entire United States viewed the efforts of the Cuban people to achieve their social, economic, and political aspira-

A lecture
for Castro

133

tions, and so on; admirable sentiments liable to fall on Cuban ears with as much conviction as Communist perorations about socialist democracy fall on the ears of 'Western' social democrats. Finally, poor Mr Bonsal was required to give a warning homily to President Dorticós:

'(7). The position of the Government and people of the United States on the issue of international Communism is well known. The United States was founded in the belief that man's quest for freedom was an irresistible force, and the United States faces the challenge to freedom which has been posed by international Communism with calm and full confidence that mankind's desire for freedom will triumph over it, as it has over other totalitarian ideologies. Communism, with its avowed purpose of imposing authoritarian rule and denying freedom of speech, religion and assembly as the democratic world has understood it, can never be consistent with the principles on which the American Republics and other free nations of the world are founded.

'Nevertheless, the United States has been convinced by its experience throughout the world that all free nations must remain vigilant and determined in resisting the expansion of Communism by aggression and subversion if democracy is to flourish. Everywhere in the free world, democracy is being challenged by the subversive and disruptive tactics of Communists responding to alien guidance and serving alien interests. It is solely against the anti-democratic, subversive activities of Communists in the service of foreign totalitarianism that the United States firmly believes that the free world should be vigilant; it would be a travesty to suggest that the United States opposes democratic ideals and measures designed for social and economic progress merely because the Communists make use of these as slogans to veil their true anti-democratic intentions.'

In view of all this, Mr Bonsal said he hoped the Cuban Government would 'review its policy and attitude towards the United States'.

Dr Dorticós replied to all this that President Eisenhower didn't understand what the Cuban Revolution was all about. Maybe the British didn't understand what it was all about either, but they kept a stiff upper lip and resolved to see both sides of the question. *The Times* of London published an assessment primly entitled 'Dr Fidel Castro's balance sheet' which is so accurate and informative that I make no apology for quoting it in full.

'On the debit side,' says the anonymous Special Correspondent, 'are the following':

The balance-sheet

'(1) The depleted dollar reserves.

'(2) The aggressiveness of Dr Castro and some of his closest collaborators, which is much too loud for the average Anglo-Saxon mind.

'(3) The left-wing elements in the Castro camp, which cannot be ignored. Leading this extremist wing are Dr Castro's younger brother, Major[1] Raúl Castro, Minister of the Armed Forces; Captain Antonio Núñez Jiménez, a former geography professor who is now executive director of the National Institute of Agrarian Reform (INRA); and Major "Ché" Guevara, an Argentine-born physician, now a Cuban citizen, who is President of the National Bank.

'(4) Unemployment—more than 700,000 persons are jobless, including some 40,000 former Batista soldiers.

'(5) Construction of homes and flats by private enterprise is at a virtual standstill as a result of Law 218, which created a new concept of evaluating empty lots, lowering their price and abolishing real estate speculation. This and an earlier law lowering rents by as much as 50 per cent have been a death-blow to real estate brokers and developers of housing projects.

'(6) Highly unpopular among merchants dealing in imported merchandise, particularly in the luxury capacity, are import surcharges ranging from 30 to 100 per cent. They

[1] Major (*Comandante*) is the highest rank in the Cuban Revolutionary Army. J.H.F.

were adopted as a temporary measure to conserve Cuba's foreign exchange reserves with the approval of the International Monetary Fund in September. The United States is expected to be hit the hardest since Cuba usually buys about $600 m. yearly from that country.

'(7) The powers of the National Institute of Agrarian Reform, which now controls the sale of eggs, potatoes, coffee, poultry and poultry feed. The prices of these items, and others considered to be staples in the Cuban diet, are regulated by the Ministry of Commerce, which claims to be preventing speculation and unnecessary price increases.

'(8) Loss of foreign tourist trade, following the change of government in January 1959, and the anti-Americanism displayed since then.

'(9) The re-establishment of revolutionary tribunals of justice, and execution by firing squads for persons found guilty of counter-revolutionary crimes.

'(10) The general dissatisfaction among landowners having more than 1,000 acres, whose lands are being gradually taken over by the Government under the agrarian reform law. None of them likes the idea of being paid with bonds redeemable in twenty years at $4\frac{1}{2}$ per cent annual interest.'

It is perhaps unnecessary to say that for the great majority of Cubans quite a few of these items would not necessarily have appeared on the debit side of the balance sheet, and few tears were shed for the troubles of real estate brokers and developers of housing projects, merchants dealing in imported merchandise in the luxury category, or landowners having more than a thousand acres.

Points in favour

However, having dealt fairly with these oppressed persons, the Special Correspondent proceeds to list what he considers the 'favourable points':

'(1) The land reform programme which is being pushed through is benefiting numerous farmers at the expense of large landholders.

'(2) A total of 385 agricultural and cattle co-operatives have been established in the six provinces and many others are being formed. In addition 19 fishing co-operatives have been established, out of a total of 60 planned by the Cuban Maritime Development Office.

'(3) The Government in Havana has distributed 1,260 tractors and 304 bulldozers, at a cost of $8 m., to the six provinces.

'(4) Lowering of rents by as much as 50 per cent has benefited thousands of tenants at the expense of property owners.

'(5) The reduction of electric power rates by as much as 33 per cent and the restoration of lower telephone rates has met with wide support.

'(6) The establishment of more urban and rural schools, and the creation of new classrooms in existing schools, has filled an urgent need. The municipality of Havana alone has already inaugurated fifty-two new modern school buildings in different suburbs.

'(7) The elimination of smuggling into Cuba, which amounted to millions of dollars annually, has been a boon to certain sectors, but chiefly to the textile industry.

'(8) Gambling at the local neighbourhood level through the so-called "bolita" or "numbers" racket, with citizens placing bets for as little as threepence, has been abolished.

'(9) There is honesty in government administration of public funds for the first time in Cuban republican history.

'(10) The Government has launched a $300 m. ten-year programme for constructing piped water and sewage systems for more than 100 Cuban cities and towns which now lack such facilities.

'(11) Although the construction of homes and flats by private initiative is at a virtual standstill there is some construction under way. The National Institute of Savings and Housing, which succeeded the old national lottery, invested $15,690,064 between April and September 1959, to launch the construction of 9,493 housing units throughout the country, employing some 30,000 workers. A total of

137

4,872 of those 9,493 housing units were rushed to completion in Havana province alone and furnished before Christmas.

'(12) There was an increase in the consumption of electric power in Cuba for the first nine months of 1959.

'(13) The Ministry of Social Welfare, which was created last year by the Castro régime, has already established six homes (one in each province) to lodge street beggars and other destitute people. At least four children's homes for rehabilitating wayward children have also been established and at least three summer camps for poor children.

'(14) The Ministry of Public Health has launched a nation-wide sanitation campaign, combined with a campaign of preventive medicine. Several teams of volunteer doctors and nurses have been sent to the mountains in easternmost Oriente province to give free medical and dental care and to teach mountain dwellers certain basic hygienic facts. The Ministry has reopened several hospitals which were closed and has supplied and staffed them adequately.

'(15) In spite of the strained relations between Cuba and the United States and the fact that tourism is now at a low ebb the National Institute of the Tourist Industry is working at top speed on a $200 m. five-year programme to establish sixty public beaches throughout the country, numerous hotels and motels, medicinal spas, yacht docks, swimming pools and other facilities.'

Much of this report is now naturally out of date; the amenities supplied by the tourist industry, for instance, are now only enjoyed by the Cubans themselves (which to them, if not to the Treasury, is a change for the better), and by groups of sympathizers from the 'West' and delegations from the 'Socialist' countries, for most of whom the Cuban Government must foot the bill. Nevertheless, it is worth quoting as giving the pros and cons of the Revolution as seen by the Cubans themselves—and Cubans, like most other people, are principally preoccupied with their own conditions.

But already most of the outside world was taking up attitudes for or against Castro in accordance with preconceived ideological conceptions. Every action taken by the Cuban Government was seen in terms of its relevance to the Cold War, and itself predetermined the actions of foreign countries towards Cuba. These in turn affected Cuba's own subsequent actions in the international and in the domestic field.

It is against this background that one must see the gradual emergence of the alliance between the Twenty-sixth of July Movement and the Communist Party, an uneasy one at home but quickly forming a complete identity of interest abroad. From Castro's point of view it soon became evident that if his revolution was to succeed in Cuba it could not continue in its amateur, happy-go-lucky way: the enthusiastic empiricism which had been ideal for partisan warfare was completely inadequate for the basic reconstruction of a nation. What the movement needed was professional stiffening, not only at a political but at an administrative level.

Inevitably, almost all the former politicians and civil servants were tarred with the Batista brush, while many of the educated people who could have taken their place had become alarmed by the realization that the revolution was not going to stop at the overthrow of Batista and had boarded planes for Miami and a more settled life. Many of those who remained were of doubtful loyalty. In these circumstances Castro was almost bound to turn to the Communists, particularly in view of his own sympathy for Marxism and his close association with his brother Raúl and 'Ché' Guevara.

What was more surprising was the reaction of the leaders of the Communist Party, Blas Roca and Juan Marinello. For the first time in Latin American history the Party was willing to merge itself in a movement which it could not completely dominate, which was held in high esteem by most of the population, which had a resounding military victory to its credit, and which was led by a man whose personality overshadowed any party label and who was above all completely unpredictable.

It was a tremendous gamble, and it would never have been

A Communist
Gamble

risked if Nikita Khrushchev had not replaced Stalin in the Kremlin. But the Communists were playing for high stakes. A friendly Cuba would in the first place give the Communists a foothold on the very doorstep of the United States, and though it would be absurd to imagine that in an age of intercontinental ballistic missiles the Communists were seriously preoccupied with Cuba's strategic value, they knew their presence in the island would have a devastating psychological effect on the United States, as it did. Indeed, the outraged United States reaction played into the Communists' hands by confirming what they had said all along, that consciously or otherwise the United States had always considered its immediate neighbours to be United States colonies. (That the Soviet Union makes much the same assumption about its European neighbours is an academic point in a Latin American context.)

But, far more important than this, Castro's Cuba offered an ideal headquarters for the conversion or subversion, according to one's point of view, of the Latin American continent. As we have seen, the Party had been singularly unsuccessful in the other Latin countries. Popular discontent had been channelled into local movements, APRA in Peru, *Peronismo* in Argentina, *Getulismo* in Brazil, the MNR in Bolivia, the PRI in Mexico. All of these the Communist Party had either opposed or tried unsuccessfully to infiltrate. But *Fidelismo*, as will be seen in the next chapter, was a far more ambitious movement than any of these, and the *Fidelistas* made no secret of the fact that their revolution was for export to the whole continent. They needed Communist help, and they got it, even though the Communists could not be sure of the outcome of the alliance. It was a complete reversal of traditional Communist policy, and one which was viewed with some apprehension both by old-line Communists and *Fidelista* veterans.

Once the alliance was concluded, however, there was a kind of inevitability about subsequent events, even though there was as yet no complete break between Cuba and the United States: President Dorticós visited the United States in January 1960, Minister of State Roa went in February, and Cubana

Airlines offered 'Friendship Flights' from Miami. But, while Roa was in Washington, the Soviet Deputy Premier, Anastas Mikoyan, was in Havana for a trade fair in which Russian manufactures were prominently displayed, albeit without arousing much enthusiasm. ('We've seen tractors before,' a Cuban mechanic remarked to me, 'and what would we do with a sputnik?')

On 4 March the French ship *La Coubre*, carrying munitions for the Cuban Army, blew up in Havana harbour. The Cubans blamed the United States. On 10 March a bill was introduced into the United States House of Representatives to cut the Cuban sugar quota. On 2 April a shipload of Polish aircraft arrived in Cuba. On 13 April the Cuban Government 'intervened' the retail stores of the United States firm Armour and Company and turned them into *tiendas del pueblo* (People's Stores)—the day after the Fidelista newspaper, *Revolución*, had invited President Eisenhower to visit Cuba to see 'the warmth of the people'. On 1 May, Cuba and Yugoslavia signed a 'cultural treaty' as a prelude to a trade treaty.

*Falling-out with America*

On 2 May the anti-communist Government of Guatemala broke off relations with Cuba, and Castro in a speech accused Guatemala of serving as a base for aggression against his country. On 8 May Cuba resumed diplomatic relations with the Soviet Union, which had been broken off after Batista's *coup* in 1952. On 22 May the conservative Havana daily *Diario de la Marina*, the oldest Cuban newspaper, was closed. For weeks almost all its foreign cables, mostly from Associated Press, had carried this addendum in heavy type:

EXPLANATION: *This cable is published at the wish of this newspaper enterprise, exercising the liberty of the Press existing in Cuba, but the Local Committee of the Freedom of the Press of Journalists and Printers of this Work Centre declares, in equally legitimate use of this right, that the above contains paragraphs which, in a covert and tendentious manner, constitute an attack on the Cuban Revolution.*

On 28 June United States aid to Cuba came to an end. On 12 June, Castro, in a 190-minute television speech, told the three foreign oil refineries, Shell, Esso and Texaco, that they must agree to accept 300,000 tons of cheap Russian oil each, or take the consequences. On 16 June Fidel Castro was enthusiastically received on a trip to Mexico City. On 18 June two senior Cuban diplomats were expelled from the United States. On 30 June the Cuban Government took over the Texaco refinery for refusing to accept the Russian oil, and Shell stopped oil deliveries to Cuba. Shell and Esso were taken over the following day. Meanwhile the United States had filed an indictment with the OAS accusing Cuba of increasing tension in the Caribbean by 'resorting to lies and slander'.

On 3 July the major oil companies refused to refuel planes of Cubana Airlines, which maintained services to the United States and Europe (Cubana's principal overseas route is now to Prague). On 5 July the United States banned all further imports of Cuban sugar. On 12 July Mr Khrushchev promised to take the 700,000 tons of Cuban sugar cancelled by the United States. On 7 August, as a reprisal for the United States action on sugar, Cuba nationalized the United States-owned Cuban Electric Company, the (extremely inefficient) Cuban Telephone Company, three oil companies, and thirty-six sugar factories.

Castro now turned his attention towards the Church, which was not only becoming restive about the turn the revolution was taking, but was also suspect to the régime because of the high proportion of metropolitan Spaniards in its priesthood. Spanish rule was recent enough to be remembered. Presumably, also, Castro's Communist allies were pressing him to take some action. In any case a pastoral letter from Manuel Cardinal Arteaga of Havana denouncing Communist infiltration gave Castro a pretext for attacking 'fascist' Spanish priests, of whom a number were subsequently sent home.

At the end of August it was revealed that anti-Castro Cubans were undergoing military training at a camp near Miami. Almost simultaneously the United States Admiral in charge of Guantánamo base announced: 'We are going to stay here. . . .

This land is leased in perpetuity.' On 1 September the Cuban Workers' Militia took over the factories of the United States Rubber Company, the Goodyear Tire Company, and the Firestone Rubber Company.

On the following day, in answer to the Declaration of San José, a statement of principles agreed at a meeting in Costa Rica by the Foreign Ministers of the OAS, the Cuban authorities convened an enormous open-air assembly in the capital and issued the Declaration of Havana, setting forth the aims of the Cuban Revolution. It was received with acclamation by the Cuban crowd, but was actually aimed at the rest of Latin America (see next chapter).

The
Declaration
of Havana

Two days later, in front of a cheering crowd of half a million in the Plaza Cívica, Castro tore up Cuba's bilateral military aid treaty with the United States, and announced that Cuba had broken off relations with the Nationalist Chinese Government and recognized the Communist Government in Peking. He also tore up the Declaration of San José and asked the crowd if they would accept Soviet aid in the event of invasion. '¡Sí! ¡Sí!' they replied. On 9 September, in the course of a television speech, he revealed that anti-Government *guerrilleros*, with foreign backing, were operating in the Sierra Escambray. On 19 September, United States banks in Cuba were expropriated.

In October Fidel attended a session of the United Nations in New York. His speech to the UN was as usual far too long, and ill-reported by the United States Press and the news agencies, but uncommitted listeners were impressed by his presentation of the Cuban case. During his stay in New York he moved from a downtown suite to the Negro Hotel Theresa in Harlem, an action which was regarded by the sophisticated as a gimmick but delighted both United States Negroes and working-class Latin Americans. On 19 October the United States announced an embargo on all trade with Cuba.

On 25 October Dr José Miró Cardona, a former Castro supporter, arrived in Miama from Argentina and addressed a gathering of most of the numerous *emigré* Cuban groups. 'We should have but one thought and purpose now,' he said, 'to rid Cuba of Castro and the Communists. In a year and a half Castro has made Cuba far worse than Batista did in seven years. All he wants is to destroy Cuba with his insanity. He is determined to provoke United States aggression [*sic*] and produce a pile of corpses.' Present at the same meeting was Señor Sergio Rojas Santamarina, who had recently given up his post as Castro's Ambassador in London in protest at Cuba's Communist alignment. He offered to 'march on Cuba' at the head of 150,000 men.

Following the meeting the exiles started lobbying for military assistance from the United States and other American countries, claiming incorrectly that when they landed in Cuba they would be opposed not by their countrymen but by Russian, Czech and Chinese forces.

Kennedy becomes President

In December the United States broke off relations with Cuba. Even so, hardly anybody outside Cuba itself believed that the break would culminate in actual hostilities, and even in Cuba the State of Emergency which followed the rupture was lifted on 21 January after President Eisenhower had been succeeded by President Kennedy. Addressing 40,000 civilian *milicianos* from the balcony of the Presidential Palace, Castro told them: 'The President who has just taken over mentioned a new start. We for our part are ready to make such a start. We will wait to see what they do. Actions speak louder than words. Our attitude will not be one of resentment, nor will it be one of fear. We will not commit any hostile action against them.' The men dismissed and returned to their civilian jobs.

However, the Cuban authorities were far from being lulled into security. Shortly after Castro's speech I asked Señor Manuel Stolik Novygrod, the Cuban Chargé d'Affaires in London, where he thought the greatest threat to the Cuban Revolution came from.

'Guatemala,' he said. 'The United States has built a big new air-base there, and they're training mercenaries for use against us. The *New York Times* admits it. Our enemies—the

144

Associated Press with its lies and calumnies—say they are afraid of our Army. We have no Army. Power is in the hands of the people. But we shall be able to defend ourselves until there is international disarmament.'

On 4 April the United States Government issued a pamphlet calling on the Cuban Government to renounce its links with Communism.

'If this call is unheeded, we are confident that the Cuban people, with their passion for liberty, will continue to strive for a free Cuba; that they will return to the splendid vision of inter-American unity and progress; and that in the spirit of José Martí they will join hands with the other republics in the Hemisphere in the struggle to win freedom.'

On 16 April Cuban counter-revolutionary forces, proceeding from bases in Guatemala and armed with United States equipment, started to land on the southern coast of Cuba. At 1.50 p.m., Havana time, next day, the Cuban Government issued an official communiqué:

Invasion

'*To the People of Cuba:*
'Mercenary troops, including paratroopers, supported by aircraft and naval guns, have landed and are attacking various points on the south coast of Cuba, between the Provinces of Matanzas and Las Villas. Units of the glorious Rebel Army and of the National Militia are already engaged in combat with the enemy at all points of landing.
'Our troops are engaged in combat in defence of our sacred country and of our Revolution against the attack of mercenary troops sponsored by the imperialist Government of the United States. And our troops are already advancing towards the enemy, sure of their victory.
'The people of Cuba are already mobilized in fulfilment of their oath to defend their country. . . .
'Onwards, Cuban people! Let us answer with iron and fire the barbarians who despise us and want us to go back to

145

slavery. They come to take away the land that the Revolution has given to the peasants and the co-operativists. They come to take away from the people their factories, sugar mills and mines. . . . They come to take away from our sons, our peasant girls, the schools that the Revolution has opened for them everywhere. . . . They come to take away from the Negroes, men and women, the dignity that the Revolution has given back to them . . . they come to destroy our country and we fight for our country. . . .

'Onwards, Cuban people! Everyone to his own job: work and fight. . . . LONG LIVE FREE CUBA! FATHERLAND OR DEATH! WE SHALL WIN!'

They won, and on 20 April, Fidel Castro was able to announce 'total victory' and the capture of hundreds of prisoners and much valuable equipment. All sorts of reasons were given by the counter-revolutionaries for their failure, but one reason stood out above all others: both the exiles and the United States intelligence service had been completely misled in their estimate of the reaction of the Cuban people. Whether or not the invaders seriously expected to be met by Russian and Chinese troops, what they clearly did not expect was the determined resistance of their compatriots. Known anti-*Fidelistas* were rounded up at the first hint of trouble, the *guerrilleros* were bottled up in the Sierra Escambray, and the rest of the population rallied solidly behind Castro.

To the outside world in general the failure of the invasion was a body-blow to United States prestige. To Latin Americans, most of them decidedly non-communist, it was a resounding victory for Fidel.

# Repercussions of Fidelismo

THE INVASION OF CUBA in April 1961 brought out into the open the deep split in every Latin American nation between those who saw Fidel Castro as a regenerator of the continent and those who saw him as—in the words of a United States journalist—a bearded monster.

It also revealed the perplexity and worry of many thinking Latin Americans who fell into neither camp, admiring Castro for getting rid of Batista and supporting his social reforms, but at the same time regretting the executions and the intemperate speeches and fearing the long-term effects of his friendship with Moscow. Most of these people also felt an emotional exultation at Fidel's successful defiance of the United States while cerebrally regretting that Present Kennedy, of whom they had had high hopes, had made such a fool of himself.

Among this third group could be found most of the members of Latin American Governments, as became clear when the United Nations met to consider the matter on 18 April. Their dilemma was voiced by the Ecuadorean delegate, Dr José Correa, who spoke of the fear of some states that

'the political and social phenomenon of Cuba might achieve a continental projection. . . . My own Government is not interested in importing revolutions from America, Europe or Asia . . . but my Government recognizes that our era is characterized by the breaking up of colonialism, not of political domination alone but by the urge to put an end to the perpetuation of economic imbalance between countries that produce raw materials for the benefit of consumers of manufactured goods.'

He might well have referred also to the economic imbalance within those countries themselves, for it is this aspect of a 'colonial' economy which Latin American workers and *peones* can see for themselves at first hand. Despite the endemic, if latent, anti-*gringoism* which exists throughout the continent, international relations as such are somewhat remote to most citizens, while the contrasts between wealth and poverty at home are glaringly apparent in all but two or three of the republics. It is this disparity which, it is believed, Castro had banished once and for all in Cuba. The beaches, the hotels, the soaring apartment houses now belong to the people; the *bohíos* were being replaced by modern dwellings, everyone is going to school. This was the popular vision of Cuba, whatever the usually Right-wing Press might say, and the man in the field or the factory didn't care what political label it bore.

But more than this admiration for the revolution's achievement there was the feeling that Fidel—as millions call him—stood for the Little Man. We have already seen how in Nicaragua the opponents of the *status quo* identified themselves with *Fidelismo*, and this was true almost everywhere. When I asked a young Haitian from Port-au-Prince's small urban working class, who had been criticizing François Duvalier's dictatorship, what his own politics were, he replied simply: '*Je suis fidéliste.*' I mentioned this to a sophisticated member of the *élite*, a former Minister who had given up his career in despair at his inability to fight against the corruption and obscurantism of Haitian politics. 'I'm not surprised,' he said. 'Where else has the boy to turn?'

In the neighbouring Dominican Republic there was widespread fear (or hope) of a *Fidelista* take-over if anything happened to the 'Old Man'. When Trujillo was in fact assassinated on 31 May 1961, the uprising did not occur, as we have seen. But the Republic still remains potentially explosive.

In the Caribbean area Castro's influence was not limited to the Latin countries. In Jamaica the bearded Ras Tafari sect, whose members consider themselves Ethiopians and want to go back to Africa, had a real if irrelevant admiration for Castro, and this was shared by more conventional *quashies* who lacked the money or the skills to better their lot by emigration. In

British Guiana Castro's contacts were at a higher level: the Prime Minister, Dr Cheddi Jagan, has met Castro, who had offered aid to the country when it achieved its independence.

Mexico was to some extent insulated by its own revolutionary past, but many Mexicans felt that the *Partido Revolucionario Institucional* had become too institutional and not sufficiently revolutionary, while others would welcome any counterbalance to United States influence. President Kennedy, it is true, received a warm welcome when he visited Mexico in 1962, but the Mexicans are a hospitable people, and it is worth noting that one of their most respected elder statesmen, ex-President Lázaro Cárdenas, has become an outspoken supporter of the Cuban Revolution.

In most of Central America, particularly Guatemala, Governments oppose Castro but a large proportion of the people support him. In Costa Rica the Socialist leader and ex-President José Figueres was originally a champion of Fidel, but broke with him in protest at his alliance with the Communists. Of all the Central American Republics, stable and democratic Costa Rica, with its comparatively high standard of living and its largely European population, is probably the least open to *Fidelista* influence.

Panama is a special case. Until 1903 Panama was a part of Colombia, with whom the United States was negotiating for the right to build a canal across the isthmus. The Colombian Senate, however, refused to ratify the treaty. The United States promptly encouraged a separatist revolt by the Province of Panama, recognized the resultant Panamanian Republic, and hurriedly signed a treaty with it.

Under the terms of the treaty the United States was authorized to build and operate a canal, and to lease a strip of land five miles wide on either side of it 'in perpetuity', which should be under United States jurisdiction. The Panamanians have subsequently claimed that their Ambassador in Washington was not empowered to sign the treaty. However that may be, work on the canal was begun in 1905 and completed on the day before the outbreak of World War I, 3 August 1914.

*Panama*

Ever since, it has been a bone of contention between the United States and Latin America. Colombia has always claimed that she was robbed—a view implicitly accepted by the United States in 1923 when she paid Colombia $25 millions in 'compensation' for the use of non-existent Colombian installations. Several Latin American parties, notably APRA in Peru, have demanded the 'interamericanization' or internationalization of the canal. Until the 1950s, when things were altered, Panamanians complained at discriminatory payment in the Canal Zone, by which they were paid less than North Americans doing the same jobs, and were given separate—and unequal—facilities.

They also complained that the Panamanian flag was not allowed to fly in the Zone, a complaint which was only partially answered in 1960, when President Eisenhower ordered it to be flown alongside the Stars and Stripes—but in one tiny corner of the Zone only. This might have mattered less had it not been for the 'colonialist' attitude of many North Americans, often from the Southern States, who tended to treat Panamanians, most of whom are coloured, as inferior 'natives'.

In June 1962 President Roberto Chiari of Panama went to Washington to ask for the redress of some of his country's grievances. He returned home with only token satisfaction—the Panamanian flag, for instance, can now be flown anywhere the Panamanians want, which is nice but has no practical advantages. What he really wanted, and he didn't get, was an increase in tolls and in the annual rent of $1,930,000 which the United States pays for the use of the canal, and a share of 20 per cent of the revenue. Panama has a reason for worrying: the greater part of her national revenue comes from the canal, and inflation has outpaced the income received from the United States.

Wherever in Latin America there were grievances against the United States, particularly where these were accompanied by a low standard of living, Fidel Castro's popularity was assured. In Panama the ruling class must share in the blame for the poverty-stricken condition of thousands of citizens, and it has been almost as irresponsible as the former ruling class in Bolivia or Cuba. But it has on the whole been cautious enough at a local level to identify itself with the *Fidelismo* of the masses as an insurance against the future—though it cannot find post-revolutionary Cuba a very heartening precedent.

In Venezuela the Social Democrat Government of Rómulo Betancourt found itself in an uncomfortable dilemma, as previously mentioned. Having got rid of the rightist dictatorship of Pérez Jiménez, it was now faced with the impatience of the Left, which is unwilling to wait for slow constitutional procedures to introduce land reform, social security and other overdue measures. The Government, however, was not only pledged to constitutionalism; it was also dependent on foreign participation in the extraction, refining and marketing of Venezuela's major product, petroleum. Any violent change might frighten away the foreigners and would in any case disrupt the economy, if only temporarily.

There have been several minor uprisings against the Government in the provinces and riots in Caracas, and the students of the Central University have been spending more time on left-wing political activity than on their studies. Both the conventional Communist Party and the *Fidelistas* are openly in favour of the dissidents and, less openly, are helping them. Betancourt, a former supporter of Castro like Figueres, has broken off relations with Cuba.

On the face of it one might expect that Brazil, the largest country on the continent, could afford to ignore Cuba, but this is far from being the case. Despite all the evidence of progress, the skyscrapers of booming São Paulo, the automobile factories, the iron and steel works, the new highways, the building of Brasilia—large parts of Brazil, notably in the north-east, are still poverty-stricken, backward, drought-plagued and feudal. In these areas peasant discontent is running high, and *Fidelismo* is growing.

It expresses itself in the *Ligas de Camponeses*, or Peasant Leagues, which have sprung up spontaneously over the last few years, and whose unofficial but powerful leader is a young

Castro's influence in Brazil

lawyer called Francisco Julião. He has visited both Cuba and Communist China and is believed to get support from both. The problem of the peasants' revolt is intensified, as in Peru, by the drift to the cities of all who can manage to get there, so that the *favelas* form new rings of discontent around all the major cities.

For years Brazilian politicians, drawn from the upper and upper middle classes, closed their eyes to the tragic situation of these people, and even the Vargas interlude made little difference. But there was new hope when Jânio Quadros, the reformist Mayor of São Paulo City and later Governor of São Paulo State, was elected as an Independent to the Presidency of the Republic at the end of 1960 by the largest majority in Brazilian history. He took office in January 1961 and proceeded to apply his 'new broom' with vigour. But he is a curiously unstable character, and the following August, exasperated by the vested interests opposing him, he abruptly resigned and took a slow trip around the world, leaving the country virtually leaderless at a vital moment.

Argentina

Argentina is another country which would appear both geographically and sociologically remote from Cuba, even though it did give birth to 'Ché' Guevara and a number of other adopted Cubans. But Perón made the Argentine workers conscious of the class struggle, so that today's neo-*Peronistas* tend to equate Castro with Perón as a friend of the poor, though the ascetic and dedicated Castro would hardly care for the company of the luxury-loving and opportunistic Perón.

All the same in Argentina, as elsewhere in Latin America, *Fidelismo* has been a means of letting in Communism by the back door where it could never have entered by the front—a proof that the Communist Party's calculated risk in allying itself with *Fidelism* was paying off. This is even true of sedate, middle-class, welfare-state Uruguay, where students and intellectuals in particular were sympathetic to Castro and did not care what company he kept. The left-wing weekly, *Marcha*, the Uruguayan equivalent of the *New Statesman*, pursued an undeviating pro-Castro line.

In Chile the Communist Party has always been powerful, particularly in the trades unions, and the Left on the whole tends to be radical. Though Chile has no indigenous problem like the other Andean countries—the Araucanos who have not been absorbed live unmolested on their own lands—there is a dangerously wide gap between rich and poor. Those of the middle class who are sufficiently well-off tend to identify themselves with the upper classes, and those who are less well-off are mostly too busy making ends meet to involve themselves in politics, so that as a group the bourgeoisie do not form the stabilizing factor which they might.

Chile has a long record of constitutional government, a magnificent police force, and an Army which keeps out of politics, all factors which make for stability. But the economic imbalance, the drift from the countryside to urban shanty-towns, the high cost of living, all add up to the problem faced by less organized countries—complicated in Chile's case by the disastrous effects of the 1960 earthquake.

The Chileans are charming, cheerful and equable people, but most of them are being tried too hard, and some kind of an explosion cannot be discounted. This situation would exist if Castro had never been heard of—but it is significant that in April 1960 the Chilean Students' Federation felt called upon to address an open letter to President Eisenhower asking him to treat Castro more kindly.

Paraguay, always the odd man out in South America, keeping itself to itself, seems characteristically to be the country least affected by the Cuban revolution or even the Bolivian revolution next door. Though economically bound to Argentina, Paraguay politically is beholden to no one. Following the successful conclusion of the Chaco War, the country reverted for a time to its usual cycle of political chaos alternating with barrack revolts, but for the last ten years it has had peace under the Presidency of General Alfredo Stroessner.

Stroessner, the son of German immigrants but speaking (in public anyway) only Spanish and Guaraní, is an unabashed strong man of the old school, regarded abroad from Moscow

to Washington as a wicked dictator. But his domestic de-
tractors have little constructive to offer, and one cannot take
altogether seriously an opposition one of whose leaders tells
one in a normal voice in a crowded hotel lobby that there is
a reign of terror in the country. Most Paraguayans are grateful
for a strong hand, and whatever the General's defects his
Government is doing one job that badly needed doing—building and staffing schools. He still spends far too much of the
country's sparse budget on the armed forces, but as a fighting
people the Paraguayans tend to take this for granted.

One possible reason for Paraguay's comparative quiescence
was given me by a member of the Paraguayan Parliament:
'We have no problem of rich and poor: nobody is rich.'
('Except dishonest persons,' said his wife primly.) As for
Castro, he is after all a foreigner, and he certainly doesn't speak
Guaraní.

Bolivia
The state of affairs in Bolivia has already been mentioned:
the home-grown revolution looks like holding its own, with
United States and United Nations help, and unless this situation changes Castro will remain more or less irrelevant. In
Peru the military have asked for trouble and will probably get
it: it is doubtful how far the ageing Haya can keep control over
his disgruntled followers now that they have seen constitutional
methods fail. In Ecuador the armed forces are still meddling in
politics, the politicians are still more noted for words than
actions, and the poor are still poor. Anything is possible. In
Colombia the Liberal-Conservative alliance is doing its best:
the danger there is that both sides may be too afraid of offending the other to undertake the radical reforms the country
needs. At the moment *Fidelismo* has a largely symbolic appeal,
and memories of civil war are too recent for any sensible
Colombian to want to risk another.

There is one area of *Fidelista* influence which lies outside
Latin America altogether—indeed within what Castro might
call the enemy gates. This is among the Negro population in
the United States. Castro's move to Harlem, whatever its
immediate cause, made an enormous impact, but it was only a

dramatic example of an attitude which Negroes appreciate. There was no official colour bar in Cuba before the Revolution, but the Negroes, being mostly poor, suffered in the same way as other poor Cubans. Furthermore, in the supposed interests of the United States tourist trade, they were effectively banned from the places where tourists congregated—except as entertainers. And in so far as they did escape the disabilities suffered by their race in many parts of the United States, previous Cuban Governments did not think this something to be publicized, again for fear of hurting the tourist trade (a fallacy, incidentally; integrated Jamaica suffers from no lack of tourists).

Now all this has changed, and the Cuban Government is doing its best to see that United States Negroes know it, preferably by seeing for themselves. Here is the enthusiastic reaction of one of them, Mrs Odessa Cox of Harlem, as reported by the *California Eagle* of 12 January 1961, three months before the invasion:

*An enemy within the gates?*

'Negroes were in all walks of life. The head of the army is a Negro.[1] There are Negro captains and Negro officers of all kinds, all the way down—and up. There are blacks training whites and whites training blacks.

'I even watched as I walked along the streets as the people passed by. Nobody paid any attention to whether a person was light or dark. I tried my best to see if there wasn't some race feeling. But there was nothing. Nothing at all. In the houses —they were all together. Negro families next door to white families. There was no "Negro street", no "white street".

'I talked to a mother of eight—a dark-skinned Cuban— and asked her what the revolution had done for her. She lived in a trashy, barnlike house. Under Batista she paid $25 a month. Now she pays $5 for the same house. . . . Before she did day work. She was the only one in the family who got a job. Now her husband and her two boys are employed and she stays at home. . . .

[1] There seems to be a misunderstanding here. Raùl Castro was in charge of the armed forces at the time, and still is.

155

'At the American Consulate they said that 90 per cent of the people are against Castro, but I don't know where they were. We didn't see them. . . . We were free to go anywhere, to talk to anyone, people in the street, anybody—and we did. . . . Everywhere we found warmth . . . for Fidel. No one calls him Castro. They love him, they love him like a brother.

'We stayed at the Havana Riviera. Before the revolution no dark-faced people could stay there. They couldn't rent a room. They could only work as menials. Now everyone is welcome.

'Homes are springing up everywhere. We went into a home we passed in Pinar del Río. It was the home of a Negro couple. There were flags on the door, and Fidel's picture. . . . Before, they told us, they lived in a house made of pasteboard boxes with the bare ground for a floor. They pay $20 a month for the two-bedroom house. It will belong to them in fifteen years.

'People are not jittery about an invasion, but they are on the alert. They expect it to come, though they don't know when.'

Mrs Cox's views were no doubt confirmed in April, when the invasion did come. Her reaction, not unnaturally, was somewhat starry-eyed, but it gave a fair reflection of the attitude of the Cuban working class, Negro or otherwise. It could be suspected that she had, despite her disclaimers, been guided towards people and places where she would get the best impression, particularly as she presumably spoke no Spanish. But I think not. What she saw and heard was what I have seen and heard, as a suspicious journalist and a Spanish-speaking free agent. She would hardly be likely to run across the disillusioned middle classes—not even, since the revolution, in the Hotel Riviera. And if a non-Latin United States citizen could be so carried away, it is small wonder if the submerged millions of Latin America felt the same way.

Apart from the rebellion against intolerable conditions, a

major factor in Castro's popularity was the attitude towards the United States: hostility towards the United States resulted in support for Castro with almost mathematical exactitude. This was a factor of which the present United States' Administration became belatedly aware and is now trying to combat: Cubans as a consequence wryly claim indirect credit for the Alliance for Progress.

United
States of
America

Mexico

Cuba
Brit.
Honduras
Guatemala
El Salvador
Costa Rica
Panama

Haiti
Dominican Republic
Puerto Rico
Jamaica
Honduras
Nicaragua

Venezuela
Colombia
Guianas
Ecuador
Peru
Brazil
Bolivia
Paraguay
Chile
Argentina
Uruguay

Miles
0                    1000

Majority Groups

European
Indian
European and Indian
African
European and African
Other

# Postscript: Revolution or Evolution?

THE SPREAD OF PRO-CASTRO FEELING throughout the Americas was naturally seen by Washington in the context of the Cold War, as a means by which the Communists could extend their influence over the continent.

However, at the same time the Kennedy Administration realized that the reason for the appeal of *Fidelismo* was the economic backwardness and social inequality of most of Latin America, and that if these were to be overcome the United States must encourage reform within the existing political structure and must provide Latin America with the wherewithal to carry out such reform.

This should not, however, appear to be a unilateral action but a combined continental effort, and on 13 March 1961, President Kennedy called the Latin American diplomats in Washington to launch the Alliance for Progress, whose title he was careful to repeat in Spanish—*Alianza para Progreso*.

*The Alliance for Progress*

The President's whole speech was couched in terms evidently intended to avoid hurting Latin susceptibilities, quoting Simón Bolívar on the American Hemisphere ('greatest not so much by virtue of her area and wealth, as by her freedom and glory'), Benito Juárez on democracy ('the destiny of future humanity') and José Figueres on economics ('once dormant peoples are struggling upward toward the sun, toward a better life'). He also linked the North American and Latin American Revolutions, though he rather spoiled the effect of this by putting the Caracas rising a year late.

How far these sentiments affected the Latin diplomats it is hard to say, but the President then came to his concrete proposal: a ten-year development plan with ten main points:

1. The United States 'should help to provide resources . . . to make this bold development programme a success—just as we helped to provide resources adequate to help rebuild the economies of Western Europe'.

2. To implement this, a ministerial meeting of the Inter-American Economic and Social Council, (known to North Americans as IA–ECOSOC but happily to all the other countries and eventually the United States too as CIES).

3. 'I have just signed a request to the Congress for $500 million as a first step in fulfilling the Act of Bogotá.' (Signed in 1948 after the Pan-American conference which was interrupted by the *bogotazo*.)

4. Encouragement of the Central American common market and a Latin American free trade area.

5. United States co-operation in serious, case-by-case examinations of commodity market problems, to avoid price fluctations damaging to the economies of largely mono-productive countries.

6. An extension of the United States' 'Food for Peace' programme.

7. Scientific co-operation between the Latin American countries and the United States.

8. Expansion of training of 'those needed to man the economies of rapidly developing countries'. This would mean availability of the newly-created Peace Corps—a voluntary United States overseas organization of young people, eyed rather askance in Latin America—and assistance to Latin American universities, graduate schools and research institutes.

9. 'We reaffirm our pledge to come to the defence of any American nation whose independence is endangered. As confidence in the collective security system of the OAS . . . spreads, it will be possible to devote to constructive use a major share of those resources now spent on instruments of war.' The first part of this proposal struck many Latin Americans as having overtones of the Monroe Doctrine, which, originally designed to discourage European interference in the Americas, had often been invoked to justify United States interference in Latin America.

10. 'We invite our friends in Latin America to contribute to the enrichment of life and culture in the United States. We need teachers of your literature and history and tradition—oppor-

tunities for our young people to study in your universities—access to your music, your art and the thought of your great philosophers. For we know we have much to learn.' This, however sincerely meant, was widely regarded as a sop to Latin American pride.

On the following day the President asked Congress to appropriate the $500 million already authorized, together with another $100 million for the rehabilitation of earthquake-shattered southern Chile.

Despite criticisms of particular points, and a certain suspicion always attaching to any proposal put forward by the United States, Latin Americans in general were pleased that the Kennedy Administration was taking the problems of their countries as seriously as those of remote European, African and Asian States, who, it was felt, always got the lion's share of any assistance going, merely by threatening to misbehave if they didn't.

As it was, cynics remarked that they owed the $500 million offer to the activities of Fidel Castro, and the invasion of Cuba the following month confirmed the belief of many that the Alliance was merely United States imperialism in another form.

However, the CIES conference was duly convened in the Uruguayan seaside resort of Punta del Este on 4 August 1961, and was attended by delegates from all the twenty-one republics, including Mr Douglas Dillon, United States Secretary of the Treasury, and Dr Ernesto ('Ché') Guevara of Cuba. *The CIES Conference*

To all outward appearances, everybody was in step but the Cuban delegation—and the word 'appearances' is chosen advisedly. While all other delegations were made up of soberly-suited, briefcase-carrying officials and politicians, the Cubans turned up in beards and battledress, smoking large cigars, and their hotel looked like the headquarters of a circus. While most delegates confined themselves in their speeches to economics or platitudes, 'Ché' Guevara made a rousing political oration.

All this might have seemed stupid or naïve in Punta del Este, a sophisticated town, where all the best places have

French names, Swiss architecture, and *avant garde* décor. But the Cubans were not trying to reach those immediately around them, or even three million comparatively affluent Uruguayans. They were relying on the Press and the radio to convey their revolutionary message, the more pictorially the better, to the under-privileged people of the continent.

The United States delegation was in no doubt of this. Mr Dillon, in his opening speech before Guevara had spoken, attempted to forestall him. Like President Kennedy in March, he bent over backwards to stress the revolutionary nature of United States policy, he quoted the Cuban hero, José Martí, and made frequent references to land reform. It was none of this, however, which swayed the conference. It was the cold fear of the delegations of the less developed Latin American countries that if they didn't put their house in order, tax the rich more and give the poor a better deal, and break up large and unproductive estates (*latifundia*), they would have *Fidelismo* or something worse on their hands, which prevailed on the Conference, with the single dissenting vote of Cuba, to agree to accept the terms of the Alliance for Progress and to pass them on to the legislatures for ratification. Since then, however, the results—compared with those of the post-war Marshall Plan in Europe—have been meagre, partly due to the dilatoriness of Latin American legislatures, and even more to political crises in the countries concerned.

Instability in Brazil

Brazil, as the largest country in the Hemisphere, was obviously vitally important to any plans concerned with Latin American progress. She had also been traditionally more friendly to the United States than had the Spanish-speaking countries. During the Presidency of Juscelino Kubitschek (1956–61) who created Brasilia as a new capital in the middle of nowhere, the United States felt it was dealing with a man it could understand. The election of Jânio Quadros, a self-confessed neutralist, caused some alarm in Washington, particularly in view of the leftist proclivities of his Vice-President, João Goulart. However, Quadros's record in office seemed reassuring, and by the time the CIES Conference met the

United States was willing to allow Brazil to act as an 'honest broker' between the republics. It was almost certainly the Brazilian delegation which insisted on the wisdom of letting 'Ché' Guevara have his say, even if most of what he said was off the agenda.

Then, before August was over, Quadros suddenly resigned, leaving the nation leaderless. Politicians of the right and centre were terrified at the idea of Goulart becoming President, as by the constitution he was bound to do. The armed forces feared a relapse into violence and chaos if he were allowed to take over without guarantees to his opponents. A breathing space was possible because Goulart at the time was abroad, but in the interim the country was without a government, and there was talk of possible civil war. Goulart returned in a hurry at the beginning of September and eventually a compromise was reached: Goulart was to take office, but a new post of Prime Minister was created, and final authority was transferred from the Presidency to the Congress, though the individual states preserved the old system in vesting power in their elected Governors.

This system of checks and balances proved so paralysingly effective that no one—President, Cabinet, Prime Minister or Congress—could take the responsibility for controversial decisions, particularly such slippery ones as what to do about the plight of the arid North-east and how to allocate the assistance promised under the Alliance for Progress. The only positive step taken by the new administration—the one already agreed on by Quadros—was Brazil's resumption of relations with the Soviet Union, hardly an action to reassure the United States.

Quadros returned in March 1962 and went back into São Paulo politics, presumably with the aim of once again using his home state as a stepping stone to the Presidency. But he was constitutionally debarred from doing anything about it at the time, and the disillusion of the electorate was such that his arrival was greeted with mixed feelings, and did nothing to resolve the deadlock in which the country found itself. On

June 26 the Prime Minister, Tancredo Neves, resigned in order to stand for Congress. Under the old Presidential system it was necessary to give up public office at least ninety days before running for elective office. Under the new 'Parliamentary' system this made no sense, but Congress had passed the amendment in too much of a hurry to notice the discrepancy. President Goulart had to find another Prime Minister quickly.

His first choice, Foreign Minister San Thiago Dantas, was not acceptable to Congress: they didn't want two Left-wingers at the top. His second, Senhor Moura Andrade, of the National Democratic Union, was acceptable to Congress, but his choice of Cabinet was not acceptable to the President. The third choice, Dr Francisco Brochado da Rocha, a Social Democrat, was no more generally acceptable than either of the others, but was grudgingly allowed because the alternative would have been a new general election which no one was prepared to face at that juncture.

President Frondizi of Argentina

Nobody could complain at this sequence of events: it was undeniably democratic. What happened shortly afterwards in Argentina was different, and had international complications. At the time of the CIES Conference in Punta del Este Argentina had co-operated closely with Brazil in trying to achieve a formula acceptable to everybody. At the time the Argentine President was Dr Arturo Frondizi, the first constitutional Chief of State since the fall of Perón.

When the dictator fled in 1955 the Army took over, first under General Eduardo Lonardi and then under General Pedro Aramburu. Both described themselves as 'Provisional President' and neither showed any desire to repeat the mistakes of their predecessors in 1943-45 by involving themselves in politics. They operated a 'caretaker' Government until February 1958, when elections were held, with the Peronista Party outlawed but allowing all qualified citizens to cast their vote.

The results were a spectacular victory for Frondizi, of the *Unión Cívica Radical Intransigente*, the former Irigoyen faction of the Radicals. Out of a total of some ten million votes Frondizi received 4,024,876. The runner-up was Dr Ricardo Balbín of the *Unión Cívica Radical del Pueblo* (People's Radicals, but a largely middle-class party all the same) with 2,549,722 votes. None of the other candidates polled more than 300,000.

Though it has been frequently denied, there is no doubt that Frondizi's success was largely due to a private promise to the *Peronistas* that in exchange for their votes he would do his best to maintain all the social measures introduced by Perón. Since, however, these measures had virtually bankrupted the country, economic reality forced Frondizi to bring in an economist, Señor Alvaro Alsogaray, one of his electoral opponents, as Minister of Economy. Alsogaray gave the population not *bifes* and circuses but what the well-fed Argentines considered austerity. From 1958 to 1962 President Frondizi walked delicately between the pro-Perón and anti-Perón forces in the country.

In January 1962 another conference was held at Punta del Este, this time of Foreign Ministers of the Organization of American States. The meeting was called, after United States prompting, to decide what to do about increasingly communist Cuba. The United States wanted to expel Cuba from the OAS, but several Latin American delegates opposed this step, including Dr Miguel Angel Cárcano of Argentina, who was presumably so instructed to avoid offending the growing number of Argentine electors sympathetic to Castro.

The electors may have been pleased: the armed forces were not. To them Castro equalled Communism, and Communism and *Peronismo* were much the same. Heavy pressure was exerted on the President, who held out angrily but eventually asked for Dr Cárcano's resignation and broke off relations with Cuba. Worse was to come.

On 18 March elections were held for half the National Congress, for Governors and assemblies of those provinces which had not voted earlier, and for the City Council of the Federal District of Buenos Aires. For the first time *Peronista* parties were allowed to campaign, on the advice of the Minister of the Interior, Dr Alfredo Vitolo, who had been heartened by *Intransigente* victories in mid-term elections.

The results were shattering. Ten of the sixteen provinces returned *Peronista* majorities and the *Peronistas* won 43 of the 192 seats in Congress as well as control of the federal capital, where the UCRI dropped to third place. A political crisis developed, with the Army pressing the President to resign. On 24 March the US Ambassador warned Frondizi that United States aid to Argentina could no longer be guaranteed if the Army took over, but there was not much Frondizi could do about it—he was stubbornly resisting the pressure anyway. On 30 March, still refusing to leave, he was deposed by the armed forces and taken to Martín García island in the La Plata estuary, and the Speaker of the Senate, José María Guido, was hurriedly sworn in as President. The elections were annulled and Congress, the City Council of Buenos Aires and the Provincial Assemblies were closed.

The *Peronistas*

In July the new Government announced elections for 1963 under a system of proportional representation. At these however *Peronistas* were to be debarred from seeking office, so that the basic question remained unanswered: what to do when an electorate exercises its democratic right to choose a dictatorial régime, as the Argentine had virtually done and as the Cubans would almost certainly do if elections were held.

For the United States another question arose: what to do about aid to and co-operation with governments achieving office by improper means? In the case of Peru, described in an earlier chapter, the answer was immediate: as soon as the military took over, the United States brought all aid to a stop. In doing so the US Government no doubt thought it was making up for its predecessors' friendship with unpopular military régimes, which had done United States prestige in Latin America so much harm in the past.

Unfortunately the United States action was not universally seen in this light. Latin Americans had criticized it as yet another attempt to interfere in their affairs, and pointed out that whoever is running Peru the under-privileged millions in the country should not be made to suffer for the sins of their rulers. Subsequently the United States reversed this decision and agreed to recognize the ruling *junta* and restore aid under the Alliance for Progress on the condition that the *junta* continue the social and economic reforms initiated by the former Peruvian Government. This step too was criticized by some Latin Americans either as a sign of weakness or as a return to Washington's old tolerance of dictatorships.

From this it might appear that whatever the United States does in Latin America is wrong. And, unfair as it may seem, this is undoubtedly so.

This situation has of course been somewhat modified, at any rate at Government level, by the events of October 1962. On Monday, October 21, President Kennedy made a dramatic and ominous nation-wide broadcast announcing that United States intelligence had discovered the existence of Soviet intermediate range ballistic missiles on Cuban soil. These, the President said, constituted an immediate threat to the security not only of the United States but also of Latin American countries, of which he singled out Mexico (though this would have seemed to be one of the less likely targets). As a result he declared a blockade of Cuba and announced that the United States Navy would stop and search on the high seas all vessels heading towards Cuba.

The initial reaction in 'the West'—apart from inevitable apprehension—was one of disapproval and some scepticism. The disapproval stemmed not only from a belief that such a blockade in peacetime was contrary to international law, but also from President Kennedy's failure to consult beforehand either his European allies of the North Atlantic Treaty Organization or his neighbours of the Organization of American States.

This latter omission was partially rectified when a meeting of the OAS was called to give retrospective approval of the United States action. This it proceeded to do by eighteen votes out of twenty (the twenty-first republic, Cuba, being naturally absent). Thus it might have been concluded that the North American blockade met with the overwhelming approval of Latin America.

*The Cuban Blockade*

In view of all the circumstances outlined earlier in this book, it would have been a surprising reaction, and in fact the reasons for the vote were a good deal more complicated. It is instructive to consider the case of the two countries which did *not* support the United States on this occasion.

The first of these was Bolivia. At first sight this might have appeared an act of the blackest ingratitude on Bolivia's part, in view of the massive aid she had received from the United States in the previous ten years. But in fact the MNR Government had little alternative. The mere fact that it had accepted US assistance of such magnitude laid it open to the charge of being a 'phoney' revolutionary body and a puppet of the United States. This was indeed the view taken by the *Izquierdistas* within the MNR itself, and the one zealously propounded by the *Fidelistas* both inside Bolivia and out.

To have recorded a vote in favour of the United States at this juncture would thus have given a handle to the Bolivian Government's enemies at home and a talking point to its critics abroad. It would also no doubt have shocked many of the Government's less sophisticated supporters, to whom considerations of world politics are remote and who would have seen a favourable vote merely as support for a big foreign nation against a small Latin one. The Bolivian Government could therefore only cast a vote *en contra* and hope that Uncle Sam would understand.

Uruguay's dilemma

The second country to withhold approval was Uruguay, whose delegate avoided even the commitment of abstention by turning up and blandly announcing that he was sorry but he had no instructions from his Government. This saved the Government from a considerable dilemma. In view of the unanimity of the remaining Republics, it is probable that at the OAS meeting the United States provided proof positive that the Soviet Union had indeed started to base IRBMs in Cuba— perhaps by showing the aerial photographs which were later released to the world.

In this case the Uruguayan Government could not very well oppose any measure designed to remove this threat to the

Hemisphere, though it may well have had private reservations about the wisdom of previous US policy towards Cuba.

But at the same time a considerable section of the Uruguayan electorate, having no visible proof of the reality of the threat (about which at the time even many British and European newspapers were sceptical), would have berated their Government for what would have appeared to be tame acquiescence in a dangerous and morally dubious step taken by the United States without consulting the other American nations. Mere abstention, however, would have been an undignified course for a country which has always played a positive role in inter-American affairs.

The solution reached avoided all these difficulties, besides being *vivo*, or smart, a characteristic which greatly appeals to *Rioplatenses*. Of course, Uruguayan Governments are more susceptible than most to public opinion, and it is unlikely that Generals Stroessner and Somoza were particularly worried about the possible reactions of their respective populations. But more sensitive Governments, notably the Brazilian, no doubt wished they had thought of the Uruguayan stratagem. (A senior Brazilian diplomat, an hour after the results of the vote had been announced, told me he was surprised that his country's delegate had not abstained.)

What is certain is that, had there been a plebiscite in Latin America on October 23 instead of an OAS meeting, it would have gone overwhelmingly against Kennedy—just as, if one had been taken at the same time in the United States, it would have gone overwhelmingly for him. Such is the gulf, not only between the Americas, but between Governments and peoples, though in this case the peoples were at the disadvantage of not knowing the facts—a rather terrifying thought in this instance.

*Gulf between Governments and peoples*

But the facts soon came out. The crisis mounted through the week to reach its peak on Sunday, October 28, when Kennedy announced he would take stronger measures (i.e. invasion) if the Soviet missiles were not withdrawn. Mr Khrushchev said that they would be. This was his first admission that they were

169

there at all. (He still stuck to the contention that they were not 'offensive', presumably on the analogy that NATO calls nuclear weapons 'deterrents'.)

Probably almost nobody outside the Central Committee of the Communist Party of the Soviet Union in Moscow knows why they were put there in the first place. The question is whether Castro himself knew, whether he was consulted, or whether he had actually asked for them. I put these points to a non-Cuban Communist and he said: 'We would have to know first what happened when Raúl Castro went to Moscow, and who said what to whom. And we don't know—at any rate I certainly don't.'

**Khrushchev by-passes Castro**

What we do know is that Fidel Castro was *not* consulted when the Central Committee in Moscow decided to withdraw the weapons. What also became evident was that he had no control over their operation (a revelation that caused considerable relief in many quarters, including Communist ones). They were Soviet weapons, manned by Soviet personnel, and under the control of the Soviet Government.

In Cuba itself the effect of these discoveries was rage at *los rusos*. This was reflected in the angry speeches of Castro himself, in the sharp drop in references to Russia in the Cuban Press (including the Communist newspaper *Hoy*), and in the sudden laudatory prominence given to the People's Republic of China —a country which could do little to aid Cuba but which had continued to back up Castro with violent verbiage as the ships with the Soviet missiles aboard steamed back across the Atlantic.

In the rest of Latin America it was not Khrushchev's but Castro's prestige which suffered a sudden drop. This was particularly true among the younger non-Communist intelligentsia, who had seen in *Fidelismo* a native alternative to both *yanqui* imperialism and alien communism. Now they felt that Castro, no doubt unwittingly, had become an agent of the latter and forfeited a great part of his right to be considered an independent Latin American leader. As has been seen, the Social Democratic leaders of Latin America had reached this conclusion some time before, but they were now joined in their disillusion by the hitherto tolerant governments of Mexico and Brazil.

It is impossible to say, without conducting a continent-wide Gallup Poll, what precise effect all this has had on the *indios* and the *campesinos* and the unskilled urban workers who had hitherto put their faith in Fidel, but in the long run it is bound to raise doubts in their minds, even if only because like every-one else they want themselves and their children to survive, and resent the introduction into the Americas of missiles pointed towards them rather than away from them—and in a Latin American country too.

Nevertheless, this does not mean that Latin Americans are suddenly going to regard the United States as a saviour and ally. The Guido Government in Argentina, by gratuitously offering two of its destroyers to assist in the blockade of Cuba, was obviously motivated largely by considerations of national prestige, like President de Gaulle insisting on nuclear weapons for France, but to most Latin Americans—including many Argentines—it looked not only silly but made the Argentine Government appear to be a *chupamedias*, a graphic Spanish term meaning literally 'sock-sucker'.

All this is liable to increase local support for genuinely home-grown movements, *Peronismo*, *Aprismo*, MNR. When I met Dr Haya de la Torre at the height of the October crisis he was confident of being to able to ally these forces with those of the moderate left in Costa Rica and Venezuela in a non-violent Socialist movement throughout the continent—a return, in fact, to all of APRA's original aims except its original violent anti-gringoism.

The Communists themselves agree that this may be a possible result, but they view it with equanimity. According to their view, derived from Marxist-Leninist theory, such nationalist-leftist régimes follow economic and political colonialism as inevitably as in more highly developed com-munities feudalism is followed by capitalism. But equally, with historical inevitability, both are destined to lead to

Long-term consequences

socialism in the sense in which the Communist Party under-stands it.

The Chinese Communist Party of course is far from sharing this comfortable willingness to wait. The allegedly inscrutable Orientals are impatient, and only too willing to risk an ex-plosion if it will hasten matters. It was a *Chinese* Communist in Cuba who said to me of the *Fidelistas*: 'These are the most exasperating people I've ever met: they never get anything *done*.' The Russians on their part are more liable to be worried that, in their admittedly muddled but impulsive fashion, the Cubans may go too far.

But the Chinese, the Russians and the North Americans, whatever their other differences, are united (at an informed level) on one thing—the ideological if not necessarily strategic importance of Latin America at a time when change is inevi-table. Of the three great Powers, the United States, as an American nation, is naturally the most concerned. And Western European countries, allied by treaty to the United States, must share this concern.

A conflict of civilizations

The basic problem of the Western Hemisphere is that two superficially similar but fundamentally different civilizations are sharing a continent between them. It is all very well for President Kennedy to equate Philadelphia in 1776 with Caracas in 1810 (or even 1811 if he likes), and to cite Thomas Jefferson and George Washington in the same breath as Simón Bolívar and José de San Martín, but if this book has done nothing else it has surely shown the falseness of this analogy.

The Latin American revolution, from 1810 until now, has stemmed from quite other causes than the United States revo-lution, and totally different societies have grown up on either side of the Río Bravo. In addition to this, while North America is the richest area in the world, despite its pockets of poverty, South and Central America are among the poorest, despite their potential riches and their islands of wealth. This alone is enough to cause misunderstanding and resentment, particularly in view of the pride of the Latins and the inability of the well-meaning North Americans to understand why they are not loved.

# Postscript: Revolution or Evolution?

Yet there is no doubt that Latin America *is* passing through a phase in which, for the time being, it needs outside assistance, and even less doubt that if it does not both receive assistance and put its own twenty houses in order it faces a human tragedy of over-population, under-nourishment, and social upheaval.

What is the answer? There is no single formula which could apply to Haiti and Argentina, to Brazil and Peru. But perhaps a first step would be for the United States to forget that Latin Americans are next-door neighbours, to stop pretending they are brothers, to give up judging their actions by North American standards, and to start treating them as just as foreign as Europeans or Arabs or Africans or Asians or anyone else with whom the United States must deal in an ever-shrinking world.

This would at least bring a breath of fresh air and reality into what has until now been an entirely artificial situation. If the United States fears that such a reappraisal, involving the dismantling of the Inter-American apparatus, would leave a vacuum wide open to the communists, the answer is that the present system has done nothing to stop the spread of communism and has in some ways facilitated it. The OAS, in so far as it has had any effect at all, has if anything hardened the Cuban attitude towards the Inter-American system as now constituted.

What then to put in its place? In the first chapter it was pointed out that Latin America was not the only part of the world to go through the kind of social, political and economic upheaval which it is now experiencing, but which the United States has never experienced in quite the same way. The problems of Latin America are world problems, and must be seen in a world context and not a narrowly hemispheric one. All dealings with Latin America on a continental basis should therefore be dealt with by international agencies.

Many of these, such as the World Health Organization, the Food and Agriculture Organization and the United Nations International Children's Emergency Fund are already doing a good job there, but they are handicapped by lack of funds. If the United States Government wishes to contribute millions of dollars to continental well-being, it could do so through such agencies (as in many ways it already does) and the Latin Americans would not be tempted to regard such aid with suspicion. Change must come, but the Alliance for Progress is not the way.

## POPULATION: NUMBERS AND ORIGIN

| Country | Population | Dominant racial influence | Majority groups | Minority groups |
|---|---|---|---|---|
| Argentina | 20,000,000 | Spanish Italian | Spanish Italian | British German Jewish Syrio-Lebanese Other |
| Bolivia | 3,000,000 | Spanish | Indian | |
| Brazil | 66,000,000 | Portuguese | Portuguese Negro Mixed | Indian Japanese Jewish German Syrio-Lebanese |
| Chile | 7,000,000 | Spanish | Spanish | Indian British Jugoslav German |
| Colombia | 13,000,000 | Spanish | Spanish Mixed | Negro Indian Other |
| Costa Rica | 1,200,000 | Spanish | Spanish | Negro |
| Cuba | 6,000,000 | Spanish | Spanish Negro Mixed | |
| Dominican Republic | 3,000,000 | Spanish | Spanish Negro | |
| Ecuador | 4,000,000 | Spanish | Spanish Indian | Negro |
| Guatemala | 3,000,000 | Spanish | Indian | Negro |
| Haiti | 4,000,000 | Negro | Negro | |
| Honduras | 2,000,000 | Spanish | Spanish Indian | Negro |
| Mexico | 35,000,000 | Spanish | Indian Mixed | German |
| Nicaragua | 1,500,000 | Spanish | Indian Mixed | Negro |
| Panama | 1,000,000 | Spanish | Negro | Indian |
| Paraguay | 1,500,000 | Indian | Indian | |
| Peru | 10,000,000 | Spanish | Indian Mixed | Negro Chinese Japanese German |
| Salvador (El) | 2,000,000 | Spanish | Spanish Mixed | |
| Uruguay | 3,000,000 | Spanish | Spanish | Italian British Jewish Negro |
| Venezuela | 6,000,000 | Spanish | Spanish Mixed | Italian Negro Other |

# Glossary

(*except where otherwise stated expressions are Spanish*)

*Acriollado*, adj. Creolized from s. *Criollo*. Used of immigrants of non-Iberian stock who have become assimilated in Latin America.

*Affranchi*, s. and adj. (French). Used in colonial Saint-Domingue (Haiti), to describe free Negroes and *mulattres*.

*Aprista*, s. Member of APRA (*Alianza Popular Revolucionaria Americana*), Peruvian political movement.

*Audiencia*. s. Spanish colonial administrative unit, at lower level than Viceroyalty.

*Barbudo*, s. and adj. Bearded man, bearded. Used to describe soldiers of Cuban Twenty-Sixth of July Movement.

*Blanco*, adj. White. Name given to describe supporters of one side in Uruguayan civil wars in nineteenth century. Now the name of one of Uruguay's two major political parties.

*Bogotazo, el.* s. Popular uprising in Bogotá, Colombia, on 9 April 1948, following the murder of dissident Liberal leader Jorge Eliecer Gaitán.

*Bohío*, s. Simple dwelling of Cuban peasant. The Revolutionary Government is now replacing these with modern housing.

*Cabildo*, s. Lit. Town Hall, but used to describe local legislative assemblies in Spanish colonies.

*Campesino*, s. Countryman, peasant.

*Caraqueño*, s. Citizen of Caracas, Venezuela.

*Castillo*, s. Castle.

*Caudillismo*, s. Rule by *Caudillos*.

*Caudillo*, s. Non-elective national or regional leader, comparable to Chinese war-lord. Also title curiously chosen by General Franco, Spanish Chief of State.

*Chupamedias*. s. Lit. Socksucker. Bootlicker.

*Colono*, s. Tenant farmer in Argentina and elsewhere, in contradistinction to *Peón*.

*Colorado*, adj. Red. Name given to Uruguayan party opposing the *Blancos*. Both were originally named from the favours worn by troops before uniforms became standardized. The Italian patriot Garibaldi, who fought in Uruguay's wars of independence, later adopted the *Colorados'* red shirts for his movement in Italy. The name has also been taken by political movements in Paraguay and elsewhere. Not to be confused with *Rojo*, also meaning Red, which is applied to the communists, though not by themselves.

*Criollo*, s. Creole. Originally defined as European born in the Americas, it now has general sense of 100 per cent local, genuinely national. In Haiti today *Créole* is name given to French dialect spoken by most Haitians, and in Trinidad *Creole* refers to a person of French descent.

*Defensa, la*, s. Lit. Defence. Successful defence of Buenos Aires in 1807 by local citizens against British.

*Elite*, s. (French). Haitian upper and middle classes, mostly *mulattres*.

*Encomendero*, s. Spanish settler given grant of land in American colonies by Madrid, on condition he looked after spiritual and social welfare of native *indios*. The condition was usually ignored.

*Estado Novo*, s. (Portuguese). Brazilian constitution introduced by President Getulio Vargas (1930–45), characterized by strong Executive and emphasis on workers' rights. Apart from authoritarian structure it had little in common with Portuguese system of same name.

*Favela*, s. (Portuguese). Brazilian shanty-town, or dwelling therein.

*Frigorífico*, s. Plant for freezing and packing meat for export.

*Gaucho*, s. (Spanish and Portuguese). Formerly independent mounted cowhand working for *estancias* and *fazendas* in River Plate countries and Southern Brazil. Today often used erroneously for any rural worker in traditional garb. The real *gaucho* disappeared when the land was fenced-in during the nineteenth century.

*Getulismo*, s. (Portuguese). Support for the policies of President Getulio Vargas of Brazil. See *Estado Novo*.

*Gringo*, s. Etymology disputed. Foreigner. Used in Cuba, Mexico and Central America almost exclusively for North Americans, on the West Coast of South America, also for North Europeans, and in Argentina and Uruguay for (*a*) fair-haired people and (*b*) Italian immigrants.

*Godo*, s. Literally Goth. Used in Colombia for Conservatives, landowners, white people, Spaniards.

*Guaraní*, s. and adj. Indigenous language and people of Paraguay and parts of neighbouring countries. Also Paraguayan currency unit.

*Guerrillero*, s. Irregluar soldier, partisan. Often incorrectly rendered in English as *guerrilla* which means literally a small war.

*Inca*, s. (Quéchua). The title given to the ruler of Huantinsuyú, an Empire covering modern Peru and Ecuador and parts of Colombia, Bolivia, Chile and Argentina. Other citizens were *not* Incas.

*Indio*, s. Lit. Indian. Indigenous citizen of the Americas, misnamed by Columbus who thought he had reached Asia. Used in this book in preference to Anglicized version to avoid confusion with Indians from India.

*Izquierda*, s. Left.

*Izquierdista*, s. Leftist, in political sense.

*Jaune*, adj. used as s. (French). Haitian word for Europeans.

*Junta*, s. Lit. Board, e.g. *Junta Nacional de Desarollo*, National Development Board. Also used to describe *de facto* or temporary governing bodies, usually military.

*Ladino*, s. and adj. Corruption of *latino*, Latin. Used in Central America for Europeans, *mestizos*, and Europeanized *indios*.

*Latifundia*, s. pl. Large landholdings, often only partially cultivated and under absentee ownership.

*Ley Fuga*, s. Law of Flight. Former measure empowering Mexican police to shoot political prisoners 'attempting to escape'.

*Liga de Camponeses*. (Portuguese). Brazilian Peasant Leagues.

*Maldito*, adj. Accursed.

*Mameluco*, s. (Brazilian). Person of mixed Portuguese and native Brazilian origin.

*Mestiço*, s. (Portuguese). Any person of mixed European and *indio* race.

*Mestizo*, s. As above.

*Métis*, s. (Haitian French). Person of mixed French and African race.

*Miliciano*, s. Member of Cuban Civilian Militia.

*Mineiro*, s. (Portuguese). Lit. Miner. Citizen of Brazilian State of Minas Gerais.

*Minifundia*, s. pl. Small landholding, generally used to describe uneconomic or below-subsistence plots.

*Mulato*, s. Person of mixed European and African race.

*Mulattre*, s. (French). As above.

*Nahuatl*. Language of the Aztecs.

*Nica*, s. Central American nickname for Nicaraguan. Costa Ricans are called *Ticos*.

*Obra*, s. Work, achievement, e.g. *Ministerio de Obras Públicas*, Ministry of Public Works; *Obra de Trujillo*, Achievement of Trujillo.

*Oriental*, s. and adj. Uruguayan. From *República Oriental del Uruguay*, Republic on the East Bank of the Uruguay (River).

*Paceño*, s. Citizen of La Paz, Bolivia.

*Palo Brasil*, s. (Portuguese). Brazilwood, after which the country was named.

*Pampa*, s. Argentine prairie, or region thereof.

*Partido*, s. Political party. Also administrative area.

*Patrão*, s. (Portuguese). Boss, landlord, innkeeper. In Brazil used particularly for large landowners by their employees and tenants.

*Patrón*, s. As above, but now less widely used.

*Paulista*, s. (Portuguese.) Citizen of State or City of São Paulo, Brazil.

*Peón*, s. Directly employed agricultural labourer, as opposed to *colono*.

*Peronismo*, s. Support for person or policies of Juan Domingo Perón, President of Argentina (1946–55).

*Porteño*, s. Lit. Citizen of any port or *puerto*, but usually refers to inhabitant of Buenos Aires.

*Pueblo*, s. People or small town, e.g. *Partido del Pueblo*, People's Party; *Pueblo de Dolores*, Township of Dolores.

*Quashie*, s. (Jamaican dialect). Peasant.

*Quéchua*. Language of Huantinsuyú, or 'Inca Empire', still spoken by several million people in Peru, Ecuador and Bolivia.

*Reconquista, la*. Expulsion of British from Buenos Aires by local forces in 1806.

*Rioplatense*, adj. used as s. Citizen of the River Plate (Río de la Plata), i.e. Argentina and Uruguay, also sometimes Paraguay as former part of Viceroyalty of River Plate.

*Ruana*, s. Plaid-like blanket worn by inhabitants of Cundinamarca and other upland Departments of Colombia.

*Rurales*, s. pl. Special Mexican police during Presidency of Porfírio Diaz (1872–1910).

*Ruso*, s and adj. Russian. Also used in Argentina and Uruguay to mean Jew or Jewish, most Jews in these countries having come originally from Russian Poland.

*Serrano*, s. Highlander, particularly in Peru. From adj. form of *sierra*.

*Sierra*, s. Lit. Mountain range, but used in Peru for entire highland area.

*Sindicato*, s. Trades union.

*Uhuru*, s. (Swahili). Freedom.

*Unitario*, s. Supporter of centralized as opposed to federal government in nineteenth-century Argentina.

*Vaquero*, s. Cowhand in Mexico, Venezuela, etc. Equivalent to River Plate *gaucho* and Chilean *huaso*.

*Vivo*. adj. used as s. Lit. Alive. Smart, clever, cf. *slim* in Afrikaans (Slim Jannie for General Smuts). There is an Argentine proverb '*El vivo vive del zonzo y el zonzo trabaja*'—the smart guy lives on the sucker and the sucker works.

*Xocolatl*, s. (Nahuatl). Chocolate. The word from which the European name is derived.

# Index

# Index

# Index

# Index

# Index

United States Rubber Company, 143
URD (*Unión Republicana Democrática*),
Venezuela, 78–80
Uriburu, General José Felix, 64
Urquiza, General, 35
Urriolagoitia, Mamerto, 94–5
Urrutia, Dr Manuel, 129, 130
Uruguay, 26–7, 106, 168

Valdivia, Chile, 114
Valencia, Dr Guillermo León, 74
Vargas, Dr Getulio, 59–62, 108
Venezuela, 15, 42, 74, 115, 116, 151
Vera Cruz, 48
Vicos, Peru, 81
Vila Pancho, 48
Villaroel, Major Gualberto, 93–4

Vitolo, Dr Alfredo, 165
Vivas, César, 86

Wall Street crash, 58, 122
Wallace, Henry, 52
Washington, George, 34
Welsh, 114
WFTU (World Federation of Trade
Unions), 104
Whitelocke, General, 18
WHO (World Health Organization), 173
World War I, 50
World War II, 52, 61, 93

Ydígoras Fuentes, Miguel, 109
Yugoslavia, 141

Zapotecs, 45